EAST ANGLIA

Travels and Short Breaks

Ronald Maddox

EAST ANGLIA

Travels and Short Breaks

David Hewson

Illustrations by Ronald Maddox

MEREHURST
LONDON

Published 1990 by Merehurst Limited
Ferry House, 51–57 Lacy Road
Putney, London SW15 1PR

© David Hewson 1990
ISBN 1 85391 089 9

Designed and produced by Snap! Books
Typeset by TRS Graphics
Illustrations by Ronald Maddox
Maps by Chris Shaw
Cover photograph: Great Massington, Norfolk by
Paul Phillips/Landscape Only
Printed in Great Britain by Butler and Tanner Ltd.,
Frome, Somerset
Colour separations by Oxted Colour Printers Ltd.,
Surrey

CONTENTS

Author's Preface

East Anglia, for those who resolutely refuse to get to know the place, is popularly thought to be a dull stretch of land, as flat as a pancake, which hangs off the eastern side of England, anonymously sandwiched between the affluent Home Counties and the distant north. This picture is wholly inaccurate.

The truth of the matter is that East Anglia is a region of uncertain boundaries and shifting character. It encompasses the classical, formal countryside of the Vale of Dedham, 'Constable Country', the bleak Suffolk coast which so inspired Benjamin Britten, well-preserved medieval inland towns of which Lavenham is, deservedly, the best known, the Norfolk Broads, the Isle of Ely, and the wild north Norfolk coast. Add to this some famous towns and cities – Cambridge, handsome Bury St Edmunds, riverside Norwich, and the impressive port of King's Lynn – and you have as satisfying a mix of history and countryside as may be found anywhere in England.

Almost everywhere one finds a variety of country houses, many Tudor in origin or earlier, some still privately occupied and closed to the public, several in the safe hands of the National Trust, and a number of others enjoying a new existence in which they double as a family home while earning their keep with occasional visitors.

Until a few years ago, this impressive heritage was seriously marred by the low standards of East Anglian hotels and restaurants which, with a few honourable exceptions, were badly run, ill-equipped and thoroughly unpleasant places to stay. Happily, this position is now changing rapidly. Existing and new owners are investing wisely in modernising traditional establishments to the standards expected by today's travellers. Hotel dining rooms and local restaurants, once dominated by pre-cooked, often pre-packaged menus of little originality, are now beginning to reflect the variety of fresh produce, vegetables, fish and meat, to be found in the East Anglian markets.

I can think of no better example than the little Suffolk coastal town of

1

Southwold which, only a few years ago, had no acceptable hotel or restaurant above the basic bed and breakfast, fish and chip shop level. Today, thanks to investment by the local brewery, Adnams, two old and previously rather shabby coaching inns, the Crown and the Swan, have been transformed into comfortable hotels of local character, serving outstanding food of a quality which would be welcome in any large London hotel. The transformation is quite remarkable and a measure of the substantial change in East Anglia's attitudes towards catering for the modern visitor.

There are several semi-academic guidebooks available which attempt to document the whole of East Anglia, listing the many various attributes of Essex, Suffolk, Cambridgeshire and Norfolk. This is not one of them. Like the other books in this series, this provides a personal and selective introduction to the principal pleasures of the region and how they may be enjoyed by the modern independent traveller who often has only a few days at his or her disposal.

For the purpose of this book I have divided the region into six separate areas of interest, each of which might occupy a weekend or longer. The principal sights of the areas are described, with suggestions for excursions and an idea of how much time might be sensibly allotted for additional visits. However pleasant the sights, nothing is more tedious for the time-pressed traveller than to waste days at poor hotels and money in bad restaurants, so, at the end of each section, there is a list of recommended places to stay and eat. Wherever possible, I have suggested places where local food and drink can be tasted. These are followed by listings of historic houses, gardens, and other potential sights and activities.

Several of these areas can be combined to provide extended itineraries, or you may choose to use them simply as guides for weekend breaks. This division of the region is wholly of my own making, designed to make sense to the busy traveller. At times the breakdown fails to follow the more rigorous boundary lines of local authorities, but I have attempted to draw borders which group together places of similar, linked character. Inevitably, this approach fails to cover some spots of less general interest which fall between the areas described, but, to the newcomer, it seems to me more useful to provide a selective, immediately accessible introduction rather than an all-embracing, all-confusing comprehensive work of record, of which several already exist. I should admit candidly, however, that Essex, East Anglia's most southerly county, gets short shrift here. Much of the county has been suburbanised by its proximity to London and is of little interest. Those unmentioned areas of interest which remain, such as

Finchingfield, Maldon and Great Dunmow, do not fit readily into a book of this format, but are delightful individual sidetrips nonetheless.

Finally, I would like to stress that this book has been researched independently and anonymously. None of the establishments visited were aware that they were being quietly vetted for inclusion, since it seems to me impossible to gain a true picture of any hotel or restaurant if the writer is already marked out as a potential provider of publicity. The East Anglian Tourist Board was extremely helpful in providing source material, as were many individual tourist offices encountered during my travels. Tourist information centres are, in most cases, extremely useful funds of local knowledge and, when encountered, are always worth a few minutes of the curious traveller's time. Every effort has been made to check the accuracy of opening times of establishments mentioned in these listings, but these details do change with time and should be confirmed by telephone if essential.

1 The Faces of East Anglia

East Anglia is a geographical generalisation, not a formally established part of Great Britain. Its shape may be immediately recognisable on any map of the country, but its precise borders remain indefinable. For the sake of modern convenience, the region is deemed to consist of Essex, Suffolk, Cambridgeshire and Norfolk, a vast sweep of land running from the north bank of the Thames to the Wash. For the traveller, the region is, perhaps, better defined by the images it summons: the colleges of Cambridge, grizzled by age, flat wastes of fenland, fine old market towns, gently rolling countryside and the changeable coast, from the eery wastes of Dunwich in Suffolk to the garishness of Great Yarmouth and the more sedate pleasures of Cromer and the north Norfolk shore.

The spread of modern British provincial life is encompassed here, in the sophisticated academic, urban culture of Cambridge as much as the bucolic, uncluttered lives of small rural communities which remain as isolated today as they were a century ago. East Anglia has been marked by the 20th century. Busy trunk roads now choke the traditional routes to its busy ports, and American airforce aircraft scream over idyllic countryside from the bases they occupy on the flat fenland. The spread of the London commuter along improved rail links has brought a new sophistication to those cities within commuting distance of the capital. But the region has not been swept into the spiritual suburbia of the Home Counties, forever looking towards the Thames for inspiration.

History

The first men to occupy East Anglia inhabited a land much changed from the countryside of today. In prehistoric times, the principal thoroughfare of the region was the Icknield Way, along the line of a chalk ridge running from Norfolk to Dorset. Beyond it lay the boggy fens, discouraging friendly and hostile visitor alike. The Isle of Ely was an island surrounded, not by water, but by fen, and no less well protected for that. The difficulties of crossing and protecting this difficult landscape dictated the sites of its principal towns. Rare areas of high, dry ground were the obvious sites for fortified settlements, while at Cambridge, which offered one of the safest crossings of the River Cam, the Romans built a fort and bridge for the use and protection of two of their most important new roads, one running east to Colchester, the second running to Winchester and the other towns in the south west of their newly conquered kingdom. Colchester was an important Roman settlement for the region, established before the development of London had begun. It was the Romans who first sought to drain the fens to make them more passable and useful for agriculture. The Colchester settlement was razed in the first century by the forces of Boadicea (Boudicca) in the first stage of a revolt which came close to ending Roman domination only a few decades after it had begun. The Queen's tribe, the Iceni, were East Anglians, and an excavation and reconstruction of an Iceni settlement may be seen today at Cockley Cley near Swaffham.

The end of the Roman occupation in the 4th century was followed by colonisation by the Anglo-Saxons and the formation of a small kingdom which fought the neighbouring states of Mercia and Wessex, and suffered occasional attacks from itinerant Viking forces. The Norman invasion of 1066 subdued and unified most of England, but the fens provided cover for the last Saxon leader, Hereward the Wake, to lead a minor campaign of resistance until he was betrayed by the monks of Ely. Hereward's use of Ely as a base led to the Norman plundering of the island's abbey and their subsequent commissioning of the great cathedral there today.

In the east of the region and on the Wash, sea trade with the Continent had been active since the earliest times, since the route from this coast offered the shortest and most reliable passage to Europe from central Britain. Dunwich, near Southwold, now lost beneath the sea, was once one of the richest ports in England, and King's Lynn still possesses a fine warehouse used by the Hanseatic League, the north German confederation of ports which dominated much of North Sea trade in the 15th century.

Cambridge grew as a university city from the 13th century onwards, soon rivalling Oxford for the fame of its learning. The majority of today's colleges were founded between the 13th and 16th centuries. One of its many famous pupils was the East Anglian Oliver Cromwell, who attended Sidney Sussex College for a year, and much of the plotting and dissent preceding the Civil War took place in the ancient coaching inns which still carry on their trade in many of the region's High Streets. Cromwell is identified with many places in East Anglia, and his former home in Ely. Sympathies in the region generally fell on the side of the Parliamentarians; professed Royalists led dangerous lives during the war years. Colchester suffered a famous siege after it was occupied by the King's forces and surrounded by a Roundhead army led by Thomas, Lord Fairfax. Soldiers and townspeople alike were reduced to eating cats and dogs and making bread from dried peas as the siege wore on. After the inevitable surrender, several of the Royalist leaders were executed, the town fined heavily, and many innocent were dead from the constant bombardments which destroyed nearly 200 houses and part of the town walls.

The drainage of the fens began in earnest in the 17th century when the Dutch experts were employed to build wind-driven pumping stations and cut new drainage channels. Thousands of acres of grazing land were reclaimed. Today they are drained by modern electric pumps, though a few sail-driven devices remain.

The 18th and 19th centuries saw East Anglia develop the face which we know today, as an agricultural region of beautiful countryside and

prosperous market towns. Much of that modern image stems from the paintings of Gainsborough and Constable which depicted idyllic rural landscapes. Gainsborough was born in Sudbury in 1727, and later lived in Ipswich. Though best known for his portraits, he was also a skilled landscape painter. Constable was born in East Bergholt in 1776 and attended Dedham Grammar School. Scenes from the Dedham area appear frequently in his work, and several are still identifiable, including Willy Lott's Cottage and Flatford Mill. Christchurch Mansion in Ipswich contains the most important collection of their paintings outside London, including the original of Willy Lott's Cottage.

While Constable was recording for eternity a portrait of idyllic East Anglia, another of the area's famous sons was furthering an altogether different kind of career. Horatio Nelson was born in Burnham Thorpe, Norfolk, in 1758 and attended Norwich School before going to sea. Throughout his hectic naval life, Nelson continued to profess a love for his native county, and memorials of the hero of Trafalgar can be found in several places connected with his early years. A less well known, though more influential, East Anglian lived and prospered a few miles from Nelson's birthplace at Holkham Hall. 'Coke of Norfolk', the then Earl of Leicester, was an agricultural pioneer who took on the task of improving the output of his 25,000-acre estate after two tenants quit because they claimed the land was too poor to be viable. Coke, using some of the ideas of an earlier farming pioneer, 'Turnip' Townshend, perfected the system of four-course rotation which revolutionised British arable farming. The estate is still occupied by the present Earl of Leicester and is one of the undoubted attractions of the area.

The flatness of the East Anglian landscape provided a new form of industry in the 20th century – aviation. East Anglian airfields became the home of bomber and fighter squadrons for both British and American airmen flying daily against the Germans. The relationship with the US is maintained today with bases such as Mildenhall which are key elements of the NATO defence strategy.

The 20th century has seen mixed fortunes for the region, as agricultural areas suffered periodic declines and traditional industries faced strong competition from abroad. This has been halted in recent decades by a variety of factors. Farming has become more intensive, and smaller units have been swallowed up into larger corporate wholes, sometimes to the detriment of the landscape. Tourism has become increasingly important as a source of income for areas which have seen their native trades suffer. The large ports of Lowestoft, Harwich and Great Yarmouth have prospered at the expense of the Port of London. New industries have also been established, particularly in Cambridge which today is a centre of worldwide renown for the quality and inventiveness of its high-technology companies. Modern East Anglia is, in the main, prosperous and forward-looking, but, at its best, never loses sight of its rich and unusual heritage.

Geography

The landscape of East Anglia is flat, rarely rising more than 300 feet above sea level, but varied in appearance. Cambridgeshire is mainly fenland, composed of largely reclaimed marsh with towns sited on the driest areas. There is little of visual attraction in the Fens themselves, but the wetlands do attract many thousands of interesting birds each year and are among the most fertile agricultural soils in England.

Most of the region is founded on chalk, and it is the softness of this stone that has led to the dramatic changes in the coastline wrought by the force of the North Sea over the centuries. Erosion has destroyed whole towns and remains a problem in several coastal areas. The coastline varies in appearance from the marshland of Suffolk to the low cliffs and attractive beaches of north Norfolk. Around Thetford is the Breckland, a large area of heathland, scarcely populated and now largely covered by man-made forests. The well-known Norfolk Broads were long thought to be the creation of nature. Research in the 1950s finally established that they were the result of medieval digging for the rich peat reserves of the region which had flooded as the level of the sea rose.

Wildlife

Uncrowded and largely unpolluted, the countryside of East Anglia is a haven for wildlife of all kinds. The region is renowned as one of the United Kingdom's best bird-spotting areas. Broads, marshes and fens attract a wide variety of waders and wildfowl, including such rarities as the avocet and spoonbill. Facilities for naturalists are widespread and well organised; they are listed in the information section at the end of each chapter. Bird-watching, even from hides, is improved immeasurably by a pair of good binoculars and a reserve of patience.

While ornithology may be the best known naturalist pursuit in the area, East Anglia is also of great interest for its insect and animal wildlife and the variety of wild flowers. Colourful dragonflies and butterflies are found near water throughout the region, and the Broads remain one of the few places where Britain's largest butterfly, the Swallowtail, can be seen quite regularly. Deer are common in woodland areas, and at Earsham, on the River Waveney near Bungay, is the Otter Trust, dedicated to breeding otters for release into the wild. Several varieties of frog and toad can be heard in the wetlands during summer.

The flora of the region, as one would expect, reflects the countryside. At the coast, rock samphire is common – sometimes eaten as a vegetable – and there is a wide range of sand-loving species which will be unfamiliar to the plant-lover used to inland meadows. Marsh and swampland reveal hundreds of interesting bog and water plants, particularly in the Broads. Visitors are urged not to pick wild flowers under any circumstances.

Food

From the fertile agricultural land of the fens to the fishing grounds of Yarmouth and the north Norfolk coast, East Anglia is a rich source of local food. In recent years, the region has come to appreciate the value of this cornucopia of fish, meat and vegetables, and local produce can now be found in many good shops and restaurants. Yarmouth kippers, Sheringham lobsters, and Cromer crab, home-produced pork and game pies and fine hams, good lamb, beef, pork and game, and excellent root and leaf vegetables are available to any storekeeper or restaurateur who requires them. The heart of East Anglian agriculture is arable farming, which explains the presence of pies and dumplings on many of the more traditional menus.

MEAT

From medieval times, the region also traditionally supplied the markets of London with poultry. Flocks of birds were marched from the fens and beyond into the capital, their feet frequently tarred to help them withstand the journey. The turkey, introduced from the New World, became an East Anglian staple bird, and the largest turkey farm in Europe remains Matthews of Norfolk.

In addition to domesticated fowl, the marshes and flat fens have provided wild ducks for the table for centuries, while pheasant, partridge, woodcock and quail may also be found in many other parts of the region. Rabbit, still a common agricultural pest, once formed the basic diet of the agricultural worker, often the only meat tasted until Christmas.

As in most agricultural communities, the pig was the most important domesticated beast, being fattened through the year then slaughtered to provide a range of products which could be preserved for the months ahead. Pork remains an important part of much East Anglian cooking, providing the scratchings for the dessert fritter pie, lard for pastry, the staple ingredient of scores of different pie recipes, and the source of some of the country's best traditionally-produced hams. Indeed, in an era when virtually all commercial ham is manufactured in factories to mass production techniques, East Anglia is one of the last sources of genuine home-cured hams. Sausages, too, are generally of much higher quality than may be found elsewhere in Britain, with less rusk, more meat, and unusual flavourings, from apple to sage. The small, individual butchers of East Anglia have, by and large, resisted the temptation to sell out to large combines and for quality can scarcely be bettered anywhere in the country.

FISH

The North Sea and the Wash have always been the most important fishing grounds of the area. Today, major fishing fleets are based at Yarmouth and Lowestoft, while smaller, more specialised industries, run the length of the coast, from the cockle fishers of Leigh-on-Sea to the whelk boats of Wells-next-the-Sea which are reputed to supply 80 per cent of the nation's whelks. The more individual communities, such as Wells, are often considered the most interesting for the traveller, but the quality of the larger ports cannot be denied. Yarmouth, in particular, has a long history in the herring trade, plied by itinerant boats which follow the shoals around the coast of Britain, landing to deliver their catches to waiting armies of salters, smokers and various fish merchants. The first Great Yarmouth Herring Fair was held in 1270 and lasted for 40 days. The event ceased in the 18th century.

For many years, the city of Norwich delivered 24 herring pies to the King made from the first herrings landed. The kippers of Loch Fyne, in Scotland, are more fashionable today, but those of Yarmouth are their equal and will be found on the breakfast menu of every true local hotel or bed and breakfast house. Another speciality is the bloater, a herring soaked in brine and then smoked for 24 hours.

Shellfish are found all along the coastline. Colchester has been known for its oysters, reared in the River Colne, since Roman times, and at Orford, in Suffolk, the Butley Oysterage remains a fine, family-owned fish firm, rearing its own oysters and smoking its own fish, all served in the company's little restaurant. Fresh shrimps, brown and pink, and mussels are still caught and fresh boiled in many parts, though larger shellfish, such as prawns and scampi are usually imported.

The north Norfolk coast, as well as being one of the most delightful and unexplored parts of East Anglia, has several small fishing communities serving a small number of excellent local fish shops. Cromer is justly renowned for the freshness and quality of locally caught crabs, which may be bought for half the price they will reach on the London markets. Sheringham, for lobsters, and Wells-next-the-Sea, for whelks, are equally worthwhile, and all along the coast there is a great variety of fresh white fish from local boats. As one would expect, the local fish and chip shops are frequently excellent, offering inexpensive, high quality meals, occasionally with wine.

Drink

East Anglia is not hop country, yet it can boast two of the greatest brewers in Britain, Greene King of Bury St Edmunds and Adnams of Southwold. The reason may be found in the fields of barley which wave annually across the East Anglian countryside. The production of malted barley, as important an element in beer as the hop itself, is a major industry. It is a matter of record that Kent, the principal hop growing county, has no major brewer of note, while Suffolk alone has two. The visitor to the southern part of the region will soon find the welcoming signs for both brewers, and many fine properties, in town and country, are under their control. Greene King and Adnams are best known for their hand-pumped bitter which can now be found in free houses throughout the country. Followers of real ale will also be aware of Greene King's infamous Abbot Ale, a drink as innocuous in appearance as it is powerful in character. No-one who admires English real ale should miss the chance to taste it; a degree of caution is advisable, however.

CIDER

There has been something of a revival in cider-making in the east of England in recent years. Several cider houses are listed later in the book, and all make interesting visits, with an opportunity to see the surprisingly complex cider-making process. Most use apples grown locally such as Bramleys and Coxes, not the specific cider varieties of the West Country, which leads to a light and pleasant drink, albeit one which is unlikely to win prizes among the purists.

WINE

English wine-making has enjoyed something of a renaissance over the past 20 years, and there are now several well-established vineyards – which usually prefer to be called wineries in the American fashion – in East Anglia. A distinction should be drawn between English and British wine. The latter is simply wine which is made from imported grape juice, from much the same basic ingredients as those used by the home winemaker. English wine comes from grapes grown domestically, usually, though not always, on the estate of the winemaker whose name appears on the label.

The English climate means that almost all domestic wine is white, with a distinctly Germanic flavour. The best is comparable with estate-produced wines from Alsace but EEC regulations determine that every bottle of wine produced on English soil must be labelled as 'table wine'. English vineyards are usually delightful places to visit, with walks around the vines, explanatory displays, and the chance to taste the local vintage. Low production levels and heavy taxes make the price of English wine seem high when compared with some of the products of the vast European wine industry. You may be assured that the difference is not being pocketed by the producer, who usually relies upon the passing trade of visitors to his shop and the sale of tourist items and local produce for any profit he or she may make.

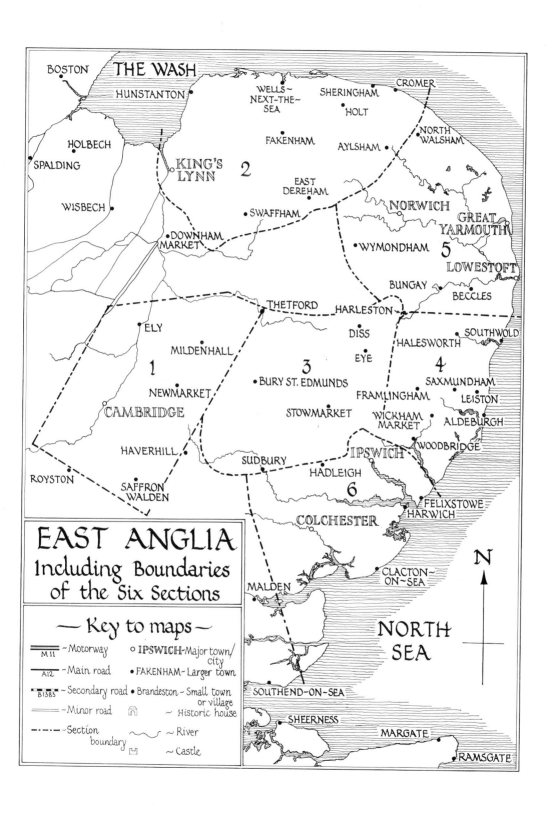

BOSTON

THE WASH

HUNSTANTON

WELLS-NEXT-THE-SEA

SHERINGHAM

CROMER

HOLT

HOLBECH

SPALDING

FAKENHAM

AYLSHAM

NORTH WALSHAM

KING'S LYNN

2

WISBECH

EAST DEREHAM

NORWICH

GREAT YARMOUTH

SWAFFHAM

DOWNHAM MARKET

WYMONDHAM

5

LOWESTOFT

BUNGAY

BECCLES

ELY

THETFORD

HARLESTON

MILDENHALL

DISS

SOUTHWOLD

1

EYE

HALESWORTH

BURY ST. EDMUNDS

3

4

NEWMARKET

STOWMARKET

FRAMLINGHAM

SAXMUNDHAM

LEISTON

CAMBRIDGE

WICKHAM MARKET

ALDEBURGH

HAVERHILL

SUDBURY

IPSWICH

WOODBRIDGE

ROYSTON

SAFFRON WALDEN

HADLEIGH

6

FELIXSTOWE

HARWICH

COLCHESTER

MALDEN

CLACTON-ON-SEA

N

EAST ANGLIA
including Boundaries of the Six Sections

NORTH SEA

— Key to maps —

M 11	~ Motorway	o IPSWICH - Major town/city
A12	~ Main road	• FAKENHAM ~ Larger town
B1383	~ Secondary road	• Brandeston ~ Small town or village
	~ Minor road	🏠 ~ Historic house
–·–·–	~ Section boundary	~ River
		~ Castle

SOUTHEND-ON-SEA

SHEERNESS

MARGATE

RAMSGATE

The Crown Inn

Traveller's Information

BY CAR

The main centres of East Anglia are easily reached by car from almost any direction. The A10 runs from London to King's Lynn through Cambridge, and the M11 is a fast link from Cambridge to the M25 London orbital motorway. To the east, the A12 is mainly of motorway standard for its length from London through Ipswich to Great Yarmouth. The busy ports of Yarmouth, King's Lynn and Lowestoft pose heavy demands on the region's roads; traffic is rarely light except on Sundays. Travel beyond the trunk roads is a much slower business, and minor country roads can be pleasantly time-consuming. All towns and cities mentioned here have central parking facilities which only pose serious difficulties on Saturday afternoons.

PUBLIC TRANSPORT

The lack of a car inevitably imposes some restrictions on the traveller, but all the main towns and centres can be reached by rail or bus or a combination of both. The principal rail services from London leave from Liverpool Street station. Train service information is available by telephone on Cambridge 311999, King's Lynn 772021, Ipswich 690744 and Norwich 632055. Tourist information centres are the best sources of advice about local bus services, and can also suggest what, if any, bicycle hire facilities are available in the locality.

HOTELS

East Anglia is well furnished with a wide range of hotels, from modern business establishments with conference facilities to ancient inns which have been serving the traveller for many centuries. Since this book is principally designed for the leisurely visitor, I have, whenever possible, concentrated upon premises which have some special merit over and above the everyday cleanliness and efficiency which one expects from today's business hotels... for example, an interesting old building, a restaurant run by the owner, or particularly beautiful grounds.

The quality of East Anglian hotels and restaurants improves annually and, in places, can be set against the very best to be found in Britain. The price of both rooms and food varies according to the whims of the proprietor. There are a number of inexpensive, fine restaurants mentioned here. Equally, there are several dining rooms attached to large hotels which are disappointing and extortionate (and, of course, absent from these pages). Travelling around East Anglia one is constantly struck by the marked difference in attitude between privately-run and owned establishments and those which have become part of large, international chains. Trust House Forte (THF) is a major owner of East Anglian hotels, running several lovely former coaching inns which were frequently picked up for a song during the decline in British domestic tourism over the last two decades. All are professionally run and, by and large, comfortable, but not a single one has the character or charm of an establishment which is managed by those who own it.

The homogeneous international ambience of the chain hotel is unmistakable and, in time, monotonous, in spite of some of the obvious attempts to maintain some Englishness of character. A number of potentially great hotels in East Anglia have now fallen victim to this increasingly monopolistic trend. You will find several mentioned here, since they are by no means unpleasant places to stay. I find their decline into the insipid age of heritage marketing rather saddening, however, particularly when one places it against the innovative attitudes of modern, individualistic hotel proprietors. One common misconception should be dispelled here, and that is the difference between the chain hotel and the chain marketed establishment. The former are owned by one single company such as THF. The latter are individually owned but marketed through a common organisation, such as Best Western or Leading Hotels of the World and will usually retain their own identity, for better or worse, in the process.

The summer months of school holidays are, inevitably, the busiest for local hoteliers. Vacancies at the better establishments will be difficult to find without advance reservations at these times and over Bank Holiday weekends.

PRIVATE ACCOMMODATION

Some of the most enjoyable rooms – and meals – to be found in rural Britain are in private homes or farms which take in visitors. A few of those listed here are simple bed and breakfast establishments, which abound throughout East Anglia and, in the main, are of good quality and value. My only common complaint about the East Anglian B&B trade is that its proprietors frequently seem to underestimate the needs of guests during the many bitter winter weeks when a biting wind blows off the North Sea and through the nooks and crannies of every half-timbered building from Cambridge to the coast. I have shivered under B&B blankets too many times in this part of the country to regard this as a rare fault in the region's otherwise generous and thoughtful small hoteliers.

Most of the entries in the private accommodation listings here are somewhat above the basic B&B level. Several are in lovely, historic houses which reserve a few rooms for paying guests and serve excellent home cooking to boot. The number of rooms available in East Anglia in this category is tiny, which is why they are rarely advertised and simply passed on from guest to guest by word of mouth. However, they offer some of the most memorable accommodation you will find, whether it is an ancient farmhouse on a working estate or a palatial country manorhouse in landscaped grounds. A number of such premises throughout the country are now members of a joint marketing organisation, Wolsey Lodges (17 Chapel Street, Bildeston, Suffolk IP7 7EP, tel: 0449 741297) which publishes an annual guide to members' houses. It is highly recommended.

WEEKEND AND SHORT BREAKS

The range of discounted offers available for those travelling on short or weekend breaks is too great to document. Almost all hotels will offer winter break discounts; many have them running throughout the year. These can be very reasonable ways to sample expensive hotels which would normally be thought impossibly dear. Almost all of these discounts do involve dinner in the hotel, however, and, in some of the chain establishments, this is distinctly less interesting that might be found in a private restaurant elsewhere. You may find it instructive to compare the price of the weekend with the discount against the normal price; in some cases the difference is scarcely worth the trouble of locking yourself into dining in the hotel. All hotels will offer you a discount against long stays of a week or more; inquire direct of the owner. The weekend packages are normally aimed at couples and individuals may have to pay a hefty supplement.

A growing number of hotels do welcome families, charging very reasonable supplements for an extra bed or cot in the same room as parents, but you should check in advance about availability.

RATINGS
Each accommodation and restaurant entry has been given a rating of up to four stars. This is a measure of price, not of quality. All of the premises listed here are thought to be worth patronising. The star rating is simply designed to give you a comparative indication of cost.

Clare Bridge, Cambridge

1 Cambridge and the Isle of Ely

The obvious base for a visit to Cambridgeshire is the county city itself, though there are good country hotels elsewhere in the area. Cambridge is an enjoyable city with good walks and open spaces. The main sights can be enjoyed in two days or easily extended to several for those with the time. Nearby Newmarket is essential for lovers of horse racing, occupying a half a day or more if there is a meeting. Those uninvolved with the turf may find little of interest there. Ely, another half day outing, will be enjoyed by most for its famous cathedral and old quarters which include Oliver Cromwell's former home. South of Cambridge, in north Essex, lies the picturesque town of Saffron Walden and, close by, the gorgeous English Heritage property of Audley End, a Jacobean palace begun in 1605 with parkland landscaped by Capability Brown. Allow at least half a day for Saffron Walden and Audley End; travellers from the south will find that Saffron Walden is a convenient stop off the M11 on the way to Cambridge.

Cambridge

Affable, dignified and just a touch lofty, Cambridge is a most likable city in which to spend a few idle days. Inevitably, it must always be compared with the great rival, Oxford. Whatever the academic arguments, it seems to me as plain as a pikestaff that, for the casual visitor, this is not an even contest. The open spaces of Cambridge are preferable to Oxford's busy traffic, and the sights more easily seen on foot.

The phrase 'town and gown' invariably attaches itself to any discussion of the nature of Cambridge. The division between those who live and work in the colleges of the University and the ordinary city resident has existed for centuries, provoking continuing arguments and the occasional riot. The University has its origins in the murder of a woman in Oxford in the early 13th century. A student was suspected of the crime, and the threat of hanging for several of those involved persuaded large numbers of fellow students to flee the city. A number arrived in Cambridge, then a small market town on the Cam, either joining existing classes or beginning their own. The history of this period is particularly uncertain because of the loss of historical records in 1304 when a mob ransacked parts of the University and destroyed many important documents. This was another town and gown event – the looters were led by the then mayor.

The first college to be founded was Peterhouse, established in 1284 by the Bishop of Ely, Hugh de Balsham. The University is a federal system of colleges, originally based around the hostels in which students lived. Colleges are self-governing and largely independent. Each runs its own accommodation facilities, dining hall, chapel and library, and has an organisational structure which has survived for centuries, headed, usually, by a Master. Masters are appointed internally, except for Trinity which is a Crown appointment and one of the seats most sought after by retiring politicians. The classic college was built around an open space called the court, in Cambridge, and the quad in Oxford. The most famous court is the Great Court of Trinity, scene of the foot race between Harold Lord and Abraham Lindsay which was recreated in the film *Chariots of Fire*.

Cambridge University is the umbrella organisation overseeing common needs, such as the conferring of degrees, not a place or group of buildings. This is why the ordinary Cambridge inhabitant becomes so perplexed when a new visitor asks the way 'to the University'. At any one time, there are around 10,000 undergraduates studying for degrees at Cambridge, and a substantial number of academics involved in postgraduate studies, teaching, and other related college work. Like Oxford, the colleges used to be the sole preserve of the upper classes, who followed a traditional route through the great public schools such as Eton and Winchester into the privileged position of Cambridge undergraduate. With the introduction of state-funded education, this has changed substantially, and the Cambridge graduate of today may come from any background, though the famous public schools remain highly successful in placing their students in both of England's most famous universities.

The majority of Cambridge colleges were founded between the 13th and

16th centuries, a handful in the 19th century, and several in recent decades, the best known of the latter being Churchill. The most recent college is Robinson, founded in 1977 by a local millionaire who made his fortune from television rentals. There are interesting stories concerning the foundation of several. Trinity was the creation of Henry VIII and incorporated King's Hall founded by Edward II in 1317. King's College was founded by Henry VI, originally exclusively for the pupils of the boys' school created by the same monarch, Eton. Magdalene – pronounced 'maudlin' – was a gift from Thomas Audley of Audley End and is, perhaps, best known for the library of Samuel Pepys.

Downing had extraordinary origins in a family who will also be encountered elsewhere, in the 'rotten borough' of Dunwich on the Suffolk coast. The bequest to found the college was made in the complex will of an exceedingly unpleasant character, Sir George Downing, whose grandfather built Downing Street in London. Sir George had contracted a miserable marriage at the age of 15 and knew that he would die without an heir. His will stipulated that his estate would only pass to relatives who subsequently changed their name to Downing and, in the unlikely event that they should all die without heir, the money would be used to found a Cambridge college. The Downing estate passed to his cousin, Jacob, upon Sir George's death in 1749, and when Jacob died in 1764 he was, much to the interest of Cambridge college folk, without heir. Jacob's widow then simply refused to hand over the estate and began a series of legal actions designed to prevent the money ever being handed over. This was only resolved when the Attorney-General himself forced the estate to be used for the construction of a new college, some 40 years after the money should have been applied to that purpose. It seems distinctly possible that the original Sir George, a man known for buying a Parliamentary seat and grossly mistreating neighbours and tenants, was not interested in the slightest in seeing a Cambridge college built in his name. But work began on the building in 1807 and today the classical college, with its Ionic columns, is as handsome and imposing as any, giving no hint whatsoever of its turbulent origins.

Several of the old colleges have lovely locations by the side of the Cam which is crossed by small bridges leading to the Backs, the riverside part of the colleges which are among the city's most picturesque sights, with a series of charming gardens, some of which are open to the public, others reserved for the use of college residents alone. I shall outline here only a suggestion for an interesting introductory walk through the colleges and the Backs which will take in the most picturesque of the colleges. Several detailed college guides exist which carry compendious detail on the jumble of architectural styles and periods which may be seen in Cambridge. But there is equal pleasure to be had from aimless wandering from one to the next, oblivious of the precise architectural style currently on show. The gardens are pleasant and always immaculate, while, on a fine day, students and tourists alike punt and row along the Cam. Colleges are private places but one should not feel reluctant to enter them. All now erect signs which state where outsiders are not allowed; if there is no such sign then you are free to proceed. Many colleges do close their doors completely during the examinations weeks beginning in early May and ending in mid-June. For an informative and more detailed insight to the colleges, book one of the guided walks organised by the Tourist Information Centre. These are excellent value and led by men and women whose love of Cambridge is second to none.

For an informal wander around the Backs, begin at the Silver Street Bridge which links the busy Trumpington Street and Queens' Road. To the south is the Mill Pool, the Garden House Hotel, and the riverside open land of Coe Fen, Sheeps Green and Lammas Land. North lie the College Backs and paths which cross and recross the Cam through a variety of bridges the first of which is already visible. It is the 'mathematical' wooden bridge of Queens', first built in 1749 without the use of iron nails or bolts. The present version is an early 20th-century reconstruction. Queens' is the first college visited when walking north; its name reflects the patronage of two queens, Margaret of Anjou, wife of Henry VI, and Elizabeth Woodville, the queen of Edward IV. The court, which was completed in 1449, is regarded as one of the best in the city and is little altered. The Dutch Renaissance scholar Erasmus studied at Queens' in the 16th century and is reputed to have been the first man to teach Greek at the University. The tower in the south west corner of the court, where he had rooms, is named the Erasmus Tower in his memory. A path from the north east corner of the court leads to Walnut Tree Court where the modern Erasmus Building, a creation of Sir Basil Spence, sits rather uncomfortably next to its older neighbours.

Leave Queens' by the street side and walk north, through Queens' Lane, King's Lane and King's Parade, into King's College. Behind its 19th-century screen, with lush lawns rolling back to the college buildings to the south and west and the lofty, ornate chapel to the north, King's is a familiar image of Cambridge even to those who have never visited the city. The chapel is one of the great sights of East Anglia and should not be missed. There are helpful staff at hand in the chapel and, for those who

King's College Chapel

require them, detailed histories of the building. King's Chapel is built in the English Gothic style known as high Perpendicular, one seen elsewhere in East Anglia but never so superbly executed. The chapel was commissioned by Henry VI in 1441 and work began five years later. As was usually the case, the commissioner never lived to see the finished result; the chapel was not completed for a further 70 years, and only then on the orders of Henry VII. There is one of the finest collections of stained glass in the world, consisting of around 1,200 square yards of window, mostly 16th-century, all of which were removed for safe keeping during the Second World War. The Renaissance wooden screen was commissioned by Henry VIII and, above the doorway, bears his initials and those of his then queen, Anne Boleyn, who was later executed on his orders. At the side of the building are 18 small chapels set between the buttresses. Over the altar is Rubens' *The Adoration of the Magi,* bought privately for £275,000 in 1961 and presented to the college. King's is famous for its choristers and both choral and orchestral events are regularly held in the chapel.

The Fellows' Building, to the right of the chapel as one leaves, is a contrasting formal, classical construction from the early 18th century. Turning towards the river there are fine views of the Backs and the attractive 17th-century bridge of neighbouring Clare College. Clare is the second oldest college, founded in 1326 as University Hall. Rebuilt in the 17th and early 18th centuries, it is often said to have more the appearance of a Renaissance palace than a Cambridge college. A pleasant walk over the bridge brings the visitor to the delightful Fellows' Garden, at least part of which should be open on weekdays. From here one may return to Trinity Street, via Clare, or walk on to Queens' Road, recrossing the Cam through Garret Hostel Lane, with more attractive views of the Backs and the river. To the right, after the bridge, is Trinity Hall, long the training ground of the nation's lawyers. Turning left, follow Trinity Lane into Trinity Street, a continuation of King's Parade which is itself an extension of Trumpington Street. Turn left again and one reaches Trinity College, the largest in the University. The creation of Henry VIII, who incorporated Edward II's King's Hall into the new college, Trinity is entered through the imposing Great Gate of 1535. There is a statue of Henry and an array of royal shields. The gate leads to the Great Court, the largest in Oxford or Cambridge, an expanse of green with a 17th-century fountain at its centre and attractive buildings on every side. Poets, novelists and historians, Thackeray, Byron, Tennyson, Macaulay and Isaac Newton among them, lived and studied in rooms overlooking the Great Court. The race between Lord and Lindsay has since been recreated by modern athletes. King

Edward's Tower, the chapel, in which famous students are commemorated, the master's lodge, and the great hall are all of interest. The latter is the largest in Cambridge and a copy of Middle Temple Hall in London. A passage leads to Nevil Court, with an unusual design of classical cloisters and the college library, designed by Wren, built between 1675-90, and widely acclaimed as one of the most beautiful buildings in the city. The library itself is open to the public from Monday to Friday, between noon and 2pm, and well worth a visit. The woodwork of the bookcases and doors is outstanding and examples of the library's rare books are normally on view. Its collection includes early works by Shakespeare, Milton and Newton and a page from the Gutenberg Bible. Next to Trinity stands St John's College, built on both sides of the Cam and linked by the Bridge of Sighs, named for its supposed resemblance to the bridge in Venice. The older parts of St John's around the bridge are picturesque but the best views can be had from the unimpressive modern college buildings on the west side of the Cam.

St John's is the final college before Bridge Street, the busy main road leading from the centre of the city, north over the river, crossing Magdalene Bridge, an important entrance into Cambridge since the area was first settled. Magdalene College, just over the bridge, has an interesting main court dating from the 15th and 16th centuries and the Pepys Library, founded in the early 18th century with money left by the great diarist. The original manuscript of Pepys' diary, in the author's own shorthand, is kept by the library, with a variety of other books, mainly leather-bound and stored in handsome cases made for Pepys' London home. Outside busy exam times, when the library is in heavy demand from students, the building is open to the public on Monday to Saturday from 2.30pm to 3.30pm. You can check in advance with Magdalene (0223 332100) on opening arrangements.

The round of Cambridge colleges could come to an end here, since the walker will have seen most of the better-known sights by the Cam. But several interesting individual excursions can still be made within a few hundred yards. Sidney Sussex College is handsome with fine grounds and an interesting link with one of its most famous graduates, Oliver Cromwell, Member of Parliament for Cambridge before his ascendancy to absolute power as Lord Protector of the Commonwealth in the Civil War. Cromwell died before Charles II was restored to the throne, but his body was exhumed and ritually beheaded. The head was left on public view at Westminster Hall for 25 years and then mysteriously disappeared. In 1960, the woman who had inherited it over more than two centuries gave the head to the Protector's old college and it was quietly buried in the grounds near the college chapel. Jesus College, reached by a walled path from Jesus Lane, contains parts which date back to the 13th century and a chapel famous for a collaborative work by the leading lights of the pre-Raphaelites, William Morris, Burne-Jones and Ford Maddox Brown. They were responsible for the stained glass, wall and ceiling paintings. The north transept of the chapel is part of the original Norman nunnery which preceded the college. Gonville and Caius – one college, not two, and generally described simply as 'keys' – lies off Trinity Street and was originally founded in 1347. Two centuries later, Dr John Caius, court physician to Edward VI, became master and improved the college greatly. Caius is responsible for its three unusual entrance gates, the Gate of Honour, the Gate of Virtue, and the Gate of Humility. Caius saw the three ideals as representing the stages of a student's residence, entering through humility, studying through virtue and graduating through honour.

Corpus Christi, to the east of Trumpington Street, is most remarkable for its largely unaltered medieval court and a collection of early printed books; Pembroke, further down Trumpington Street, has, in its chapel, the first completed work of Christopher Wren; Emmanuel has another Wren chapel and a tablet which commemorates the graduate John Harvard who founded the university which bears his name in America.

Nor are colleges the only attractions of Cambridge. Several churches are of interest, the most popular being the church of St Mary the Great, at the very heart of the city opposite the Senate House. This is the University Church, dating from the 15th century, an imposing building in the Perpendicular style. The interior is of little note; what attracts visitors is the chance to climb the tower for memorable and unique views of the city. St Bene't – a contraction of St Benedict's – is the oldest church in Cambridgeshire, with an unusual foursquare Saxon tower. It was once the place of worship for the scholars of nearby Corpus Christi. All Saints', in Jesus Lane, has more decorative work and stained glass by the pre-Raphaelites (in the main, atheists to a man, it should be said).

There are only four round churches in Britain; Cambridge's curiosity dates from the 12th century and is a mixture of original Norman and 19th-century Victorian fancy. St Mary the Less – better known as Little St Mary's – is close by Peterhouse and largely unremarkable save for one anecdote. Inside the door is a monument to a former minister of the church, Godfrey Washington, which bears the Washington arms, a series of stars, stripes and eagle. It is claimed that these were the origin of the flag of the United States from the influence of a later Washington, George. Two final

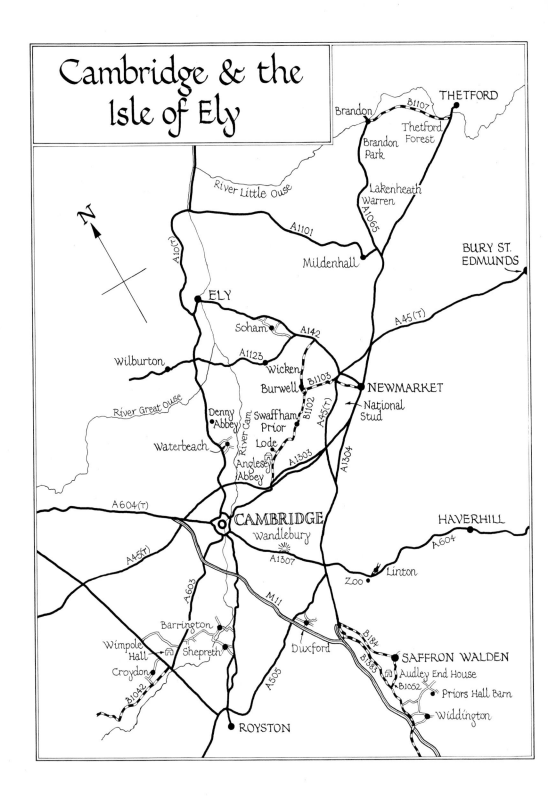

Cambridge & the Isle of Ely

buildings in central Cambridge deserve mention. The Senate House, situated in King's Parade next to King's, is a formal building of coolly classical beauty standing behind a perfectly manicured lawn. It is here that degrees are awarded in a timeless annual ceremony and the meetings of the University's 'parliament', the Senate, discuss matters of joint interest to the colleges. The School of Pythagoras, close to St John's, is one of the oldest houses in the country, dating from the beginning of the 13th century or earlier. It has no known connection with the Greek scholar and has never been used as a school. Walter de Merton gave it to the college that bears his name in 1271 and it remains the college's property today, often used for receptions though it is closed to the public.

Beyond the colleges, the Fitzwilliam Museum is one of the most outstanding in Britain, with an exceptional collection of paintings and antiquities. The University Museum of Archeology and Anthropology displays native dress, shrunken heads and totemic items from many countries, and the scientific world is recorded at the Whipple Museum of Science. The Scott Polar Research Institute is dedicated to polar life and exploration. The University Botanic Gardens maintain a vast collection of plants in outdoor beds and glasshouses, while there are pleasant walks through all the main city parks, from Lammas Land in the south to Jesus Green and Midsummer Common by the Cam in the north. Punts, rowing boats and canoes can be hired from several stations on the river – but avoid punting unless you have tried before and know what you are doing. It is much more difficult than it looks.

Ely

'The Isle of Eels' is the origin of Ely's name, and a good many still evade the angler's hook in the network of fen channels around the town today. Folk tales say that St Dunstan turned the monks of this ancient religious community into eels for their wilful breaking of the strict vows of celibacy. Ely rises gently from the flat fen landscape 16 miles north of Cambridge, the view dominated by the great cathedral which seems quite out of proportion with the small town around it. The abbey was founded in AD 673 by St Etheldreda and was the base of Hereward the Wake, the Saxon leader who fought a rearguard action against the Normans from the safety of his 'island', in reality a safe encampment of high ground in a land of treacherous fens largely impassable to those who did not know their way through them.

The Normans prevailed in the end, imposing their own abbot who, at the age of 80, laid the plans for a new abbey with an unusual, large west tower. In the early 14th century, the central tower of the cathedral – as the abbey had become – collapsed. The sacrist of the time was Alan of Walsingham whose response to this disastrous event was to reveal him as one of the great architects of the Middle Ages. Alan did not simply rebuild the central tower but replaced it with a unique octagon containing 400 tons of lead and wood supported by timbers leading to eight pillars. The octagon appears to be suspended in the air, shot through with light from the outside. It is a most remarkable feature; its creator is buried in the east end of the nave. Alan of Walsingham was also responsible for starting the construction of the widely admired Lady Chapel, the largest of its kind in England. Here one can see a series of carvings which have apparently been beheaded. They originally depicted scenes from the Virgin's life. Oliver Cromwell, who lived near the cathedral and was on far from friendly terms with its incumbents, is often blamed, but the vandalism actually took place during the Reformation when the monastery at Ely was dissolved.

Ely Cathedral

Beyond the octagon and the Lady Chapel the cathedral has a number of lesser sights. St Edmund's Chapel retains several wall paintings dating from the 12th century while the exterior of the original Prior's Door, used as the main entrance from the cloister, shows attractive Norman figures and decoration. Part of the cathedral has now been set aside as a stained glass museum, with a separate entrance fee. The museum has a wide range of examples of stained glass art, from a 14th-century Annunciation from Worcestershire, to the Gothic revival and the pre-Raphaelites.

Modern stained glass work, and early 20th-century examples, are on display and there is a photographic exhibition detailing the history of the art and the techniques which lie behind it. The North Triforium where the museum is located also has good views of the cathedral from an angle often missed by the casual visitor.

Ely, like many cathedrals of its age, is in a poor state of repair and requires many millions of pounds of restoration work. It has chosen to follow the heritage industry route in order to recoup the money, introducing an admission charge and, more oddly, a cafe within the refectory. The atmosphere suffers, inevitably, and this visitor at least finds it a little disconcerting to see, in a cathedral of this antiquity, a sign pointing out that toilet facilities are for users of the cafe only. However, the book shop is excellent and staffed by assistants who are full of useful information, about the cathedral itself and the neighbourhood.

One can be grateful to Ely's limited development as a town for the preservation of the cathedral precincts, much of which are occupied by King's School. The original priory gatehouse dating from 1397, the Porta, remains the entrance to the precincts from the south. Prior Crauden's ornate Chapel, still open to visitors, now belongs to the school and has a tall undercroft of 11th-century origins, and much decoration. There is a pleasant walk taking a leisurely hour from the cathedral to the Porta then across Cherry Hill to the River Ouse running to the south east through Cutter Lane. Turn left at the river, walking past 18th-century cottages, then return to the town by Little Lane, Fore Hill and the back of the old High Street to Minster Place. Cross Palace Green, with the 15th- and 16th-century Bishop's Palace to the left to find a large half-timbered house, currently closed to the public. This was Cromwell's home from 1636 to 1647, and his New Model Army trained in the countryside around Ely. Through his mother, Cromwell had relations who collected dues for Ely Cathedral. Cromwell, never a lover of anything that smacked of High Church, ordered the closure of the cathedral for 17 years from 1644.

Ely has its own nature trail, Roswell Pits, which begins off Springhead Lane, to the east of the town. There are two tracks, varying in length between $^3/_4$ and $2^1/_2$ miles. Further east, some ten miles away, there are walks in Lakenheath Warren and Thetford Forest, home of red squirrels, roe and red deer and golden pheasants. The large village of Burwell, between Ely and Newmarket, is an attractive diversion, with several handsome old houses and one of the best Perpendicular churches in the county, partly flint and dating back to the 13th century. A few miles away another amenable village Swaffham Prior has a real curiosity, two churches built in one churchyard. One, St Cyriac and Julitta, was built for a separate parish and is partly ruined. The main church, St Mary's, is Norman with an unusual tower which changes from four sides at the base to 16 at the top. The pair make an unusual picture for the scrapbook.

Newmarket

The visitor will know already whether Newmarket is likely to be of interest. It is a town dedicated to the breeding, training and racing of horses, above all else. If you find equestrian pursuits tedious, then avoid the place, for the locals will surely look upon anyone dismissive of 'the gee-gees' as a lost soul barely deserving of pity. The town is only a 30-minute drive east of Cambridge and can easily occupy half a day if you take in the National Stud and the National Horse Racing Museum. On race days the place is besieged by binocular-toting horse fans covered in the mandatory meeting badges. The rest of the time the place is distinctly sleepy and almost unrecognisable to someone who has previously only seen it in full flood.

It was the Royal Family who made horse racing fashionable in Newmarket. James I often hunted in the area, Charles II loved the royal stables and the opportunity to slip out of town with one of his many mistresses. Royal patronage is just as strong today, with a Queen who is as fond and knowledgeable of horse flesh as any of her ancestors.

The town is largely unspoilt, with a handsome High Street of Georgian and Victorian origins, now the home of several upmarket clothiers and gift shops. The National Horse Racing Museum, in a Georgian house here, was opened by the Queen in 1983 and offers the visitor five galleries detailing the history of horse racing.

The National Stud lies two miles south west of the town, off the A1304. There are conducted tours of the National Stud at 11.15am and 2.30pm during weekdays, 11.15am only on Saturdays from April to September. The Stud was formed during the First World War and is one of the principal stallion stations in Britain, with six top class stallions. Strings of racehorses galloping across the acres of heathland outside the town are a common and picturesque sight, as pleasing to the novice of the track as to the inveterate follower of form.

Saffron Walden, Essex

Saffron Walden and Audley End

North Essex is still sufficiently remote from London to retain its own local character, and Saffron Walden is, without doubt, its finest town. It gains its name from the ancient industry of saffron-growing, now an art largely confined to the Mediterranean and near East. Into the Middle Ages saffron was a busy and lucrative industry for the town. The rare, golden spice comes from the dried stigmas of the saffron crocus, crocus sativus. Thousands of flowers and hours of labour are required to make a small quantity of true saffron, hence its high price through the ages. Specialists estimate that at least 20,000 stigmas are required to produce one kilo of modern saffron. It was high labour costs that finally put paid to saffron production in the 18th century. At the town museum the saffron crocus can be seen flowering in the autumn.

Saffron Walden itself is primarily a place for wandering. The streets are largely medieval and there are many notable examples of 'pargeting', a form of outside wall decoration peculiar to East Anglia. Pargeting is a kind of sculpture in plaster, varying from basic geometric patterns in the simplest of examples to complete heraldic coats of arms on large residences. The Sun Inn, reputed to have been used as Cromwell's

31

headquarters for a time, is an instance of pargeting taken to extremes. The decorations in plaster cover most of the exterior and those over the wagon way recount an old local legend of how an East Anglian carter killed the Giant of Wisbech on the road to King's Lynn. On the common is an unusual earth maze of some 120 feet in diameter. The lines of the maze are dug a few feet into the earth and are followed on foot; most people find their way through in around ten minutes. In the grounds of the town museum lie the ruins of the Norman Castle which once protected the town.

Audley End is the stately home of Saffron Walden and one which the casual traveller could miss quite easily since it lies on the quiet B1383 a mile to the west of the town. There is a spectacular view of the palatial frontage from the road and nothing disappoints at closer quarters. The house is Jacobean in origin and stands in grounds landscaped by Capability Brown. The furnishings range from baroque to classical, one of the finest rooms being the Great Hall with its large baroque wooden screen. Regular special events are organised at the house, from craft festivals to music, details of which are available from the town's tourist information centre.

Tourist Information

Wheeler Street
Cambridge
Tel: 0223 322640.
Nov-Mar, Mon-Fri 9-5; Apr-June and Sept-Oct, Mon-Fri 9-6; all year, Sats 9-6; May-Sept, Suns & Bank Hols 10.30-3.30. Guided tours.

1 Market Place
Saffron Walden
Tel: 0799 24282
Apr-Oct, Mon-Sat 9.30-4.30; Nov-Mar, Mon-Sat 10-4. Guided tours.

Hotels

University Arms Hotel
Regent Street
Cambridge
Tel: 0223 351241
Traditional hotel close to the city centre. Popular, booking advisable.
Rooms: 112
Credit cards: Visa, Diners, Amex
Rating ★★★

Lensfield Hotel
53 Lensfield Road
Cambridge
Tel: 0223 355017/312905
Reasonably priced private hotel, centrally located.
Rooms: 26
Credit cards: Access, Visa, Diners, Amex
Rating ★★

Centennial Hotel
63-69 Hills Road
Cambridge
Tel: 0223 314652
Family-run establishment close to colleges.
Rooms: 22
Credit cards: Access, Visa, Diners, Amex
Rating ★★★

Arundel House Hotel
53 Chesterton Road
Cambridge
Tel: 0223 67701
Reasonably-priced in attractive location overlooking the Cam.
Rooms: 81
Credit cards: Access, Visa, Diners, Amex
Rating ★★★

Garden House
Granta Place, off Mill Lane
Cambridge
Tel: 0223 63421
The city's main luxury hotel, set beside the Cam close to the centre. Fishing and punting available.
Rooms: 113
Credit cards: Access, Visa, Diners, Amex
Rating ★★★★

Private Accommodation

Melbourn Bury
Nr. Royston, Herts SG8 6DE
Tel: 0763 61151
Impressive private house of Tudor origins owned by the same family for 150 years. Off the A10 north of Royston, Cambridge 20 minutes.
Rooms: 3
Credit cards: Amex
Rating ★★★

The Stow
Great Sampford
Saffron Walden
Tel: 0728 746524
Family Tudor cottage in a pretty village with 14th-century church, close to Audley End.
Rooms: 2
Credit cards: none
Rating ★★

Elmdon Lee
Littlebury Green
Nr. Saffron Walden
Tel: 0763 838237

Elmdon Lee contd
Inexpensive rooms in a farmhouse on a 300-acre estate two miles from Audley End.
Rooms: 3
Credit cards: none
Rating ★★

Severals Country House Hotel
3 Bury Road
Newmarket
Tel: 0638 668491
Large country house hotel close to town centre.
Rooms: 42
Credit cards: Access, Visa, Amex
Rating ★★★

Restaurants

Jean Louis
15 Magdalene Street
Cambridge
Tel: 0223 315232
Genuine provincial French cuisine close to the Magdalene Bridge. The lunchtime fixed price menu is a bargain; evenings are more expensive.
Closed Monday
Credit cards: Access, Visa, Amex
Rating ★★★

Arundel House Hotel
53 Chesterton Road
Cambridge
Tel: 0223 67701
Friendly restaurant with continental and English cooking overlooking the Cam.
Credit cards: Access, Visa, Amex
Rating ★★

Cambridge Blue
85 Gwydir Street
Cambridge
Tel: 0223 61382
Friendly independent pub with good real ales and imaginative meals and bar snacks.

Food and Drink

Chilford Hundred Vineyard
Balsham Road
Linton
Cambridge
Tel: 0223 892641
Working vineyard, picnic area, banqueting halls and art gallery. May-Oct, daily 11-5.

Downfield Windmill
Fordham Road
Soham
5m SE Ely
Tel: 0533 707625
Home ground flour products from a mill which dates from 1720. Flour sold in local shops; mill open to public Sunday 11-5.

Historic Houses

Anglesey Abbey
Lode
6m NE Cambridge
Famous gardens and collection of paintings and furniture housed in a former 13th-century abbey with Tudor additions. House, Mar 25-Oct 15, Wed-Sun 1.30-5.30; gardens Mar 25-Jul 2, Wed-Sun 1.30-5.30; Jul 2-Oct 15, Wed-Sun 12-5.30.

Wimpole Hall (NT)
Near Wimpole
Cambridge
Classic 18th-century mansion with landscaping by Capability Brown, among others. Attached farm displays rare cattle breeds and old agricultural equipment. House, Mar 25-Oct 29, 1-5, daily ex Mon and Fri. Farm, Mar 25-Oct 29, 10.30-5, daily ex Mon and Fri.

Audley End House (EH)
Saffron Walden
Stunning Jacobean mansion – both interior and exterior – set in Capability Brown parkland. Fine collection of silver and furniture. Open Mar 24-Sept 30 daily, 1-6. Last admission one hour before closure.

Gardens

Cambridge University Botanic Gardens
Laid out in 1846, with glasshouses and a limestone rock garden. Nov-Jan, Mon-Sat 8-4; Feb-Apr and Oct 8-5; May-Sept Mon-Sat 8-6, Sun 2.30-6.30.

Herb Garden
Nigel House
Wilburton
5m SW Ely
Tel: 0533 740824
Culinary, medicinal and astrological herb collection, with products for sale. May-Sept, 10-7 most days. Closed Wed school terms.

Ancient Monuments

King's College Chapel
King's Parade
Cambridge
Permanent exhibition detailing the famous chapel's construction. Mid Mar–mid Oct, Mon-Sat 9.30-3.30 (Sun 11-5 university vacations only); winter, Mon-Sat 11-3.30 (Sun 12-3.30, university vacations only).

Denny Abbey
Ely Road
Waterbeach
5m NE Cambridge
Ruins of former Knights' Templar hospital and priory; 12th- and 14th-century remains. 24 Mar-30 Sept, 10-6; winter, Suns only 10-4.

Priors Hall Barn
Widdington
4m S Saffron Walden
One of the best remaining examples of a medieval aisled barn. 24 Mar-30 Sept, weekends and Bank Hols only 10-6.

Museums

Fitzwilliam Museum
Trumpington Street
Cambridge

The city's leading museum, with collections ranging from Egyptology to painting. Tues-Sat Lower Galleries 10-2, Upper Galleries 2-5; Sun, all galleries 2.15-5.

Imperial War Museum
Duxford Airfield
8m S Cambridge
Historic aircraft from the First World War to modern times. Mid Mar-end Oct daily, 10.30-5.30. Winter daily, 10.30-3.45

Cambridge and County Folk Museum
Castle Street
Cambridge
Craft and folk museum representing Fenland life over the centuries. Mon-Sat 10.30-5, Sun 2.30-4.30.

University Museum of Archeology and Anthropology
Downing Street
Cambridge
Archeological finds from the area, and an international collection of prehistoric artefacts. Mon-Fri 2-4; Sats 10-12.30.

University Museum of Classical Archeology
Sidgwick Avenue
Cambridge
Collection of Roman and Greek art. Mon-Fri 9-1, 2.15-5.

Whipple Museum of the History of Science
Free School Lane
Cambridge
Fascinating collection of historic scientific instruments. Mon-Fri 2-4.

Ely Museum
High Street
Ely
Admirable modern museum recounting the city's history through modern audio-visual techniques and conventional collections. Tue-Sun 10-5.

35

National Horse Racing Museum
High Street
Newmarket
Tel: 0638 667333
Homage to the four-legged creatures which dominate Newmarket life. Opened by the Queen in 1983. Mar-Dec, Tue-Sat 10-5, Sun 2-5; Aug, Mon-Sat 10-5, Sun 2-5. Other times by appointment.

Wildlife Parks and Reserves

Brookcroft Bunnery
High Street
Croydon
Royston
Tel: 0223 207331
Display of rare and unusual rabbits and knitwear from rabbit wool. Apr-Oct, Wed-Sun 10.30-4; Sat and Sun by appointment only in winter.

Linton Zoo
Hadstock Road,
Linton
Cambridge
More than ten acres of zoo park. All year, 10-6.30 or dusk.

Willers Mill Wild Animal Sanctuary and Fish Farm
Station Road
Shepreth
8m SW Cambridge
Wild and domestic animals and fish in eight acres of natural surroundings. Mar-Oct 10.30-6; Sat and Sun 10.30-dusk in winter.

Wicken Fen
nr Soham
5m SW Ely
National Trust wildfowl reserve with windmill. Open daily except Thursday; sign book at keeper's lodge.

Walks

Brandon
1m S Brandon
Splendid walking in Brandon forest with views of Brandon Park House. More than 30 acres. May-Oct, daily 10-9.

Wandlebury
5m SE Cambridge
Well-marked nature trail and walks across parkland with Iron Age fort and picnic areas.

Coe Fen and Paradise Nature Trails
Cambridge
Organised walks along the Cam. Guidebooks – essential – from Cambridgeshire Wildlife Trust, 5 Fulbourn Manor, Fulbourn, Cambridge CB1 5BN. Tel: 0223 880788.

Shepreth Riverside Walk
SW Cambridge
Leisurely walk by the Cam from Shepreth to Barrington.

Other Diversions

Scudamores Boatyards
Granta Place
Cambridge
Tel: 0223 359750
Punts, rowing boats and canoes for hire, and a 40-minute 'chauffeur punt' on the Cam.

Saffron Walden Maze
The Common
Earth maze – no hedges to block the view. Open all year, free.

Burnham Overy Staithe, Norfolk

2 King's Lynn and the North Norfolk Coast

The stretch of coastline running from the Wash to Cromer is one of the most enjoyable parts of East Anglia, with a string of small, agreeable resorts and several interesting excursions inland. The principal town of the area is King's Lynn, an old port which retains an interesting medieval quarter and quayside. The A149 coast road makes travel in the area relatively easy, and Lynn can serve as a base for visiting the whole of north Norfolk. There are several excellent private hotels further east, however, in small towns like Wells and Cromer. The Queen's country residence of Sandringham and Holkham Hall, the home of the Earl of Leicester, are both magnificent estates worth visiting. There are several superb bird-watching points along the coast. Inland lies the intriguing holy village of Walsingham, once the scene of pilgrimages from all over Europe. The coastline produces some of the best fish and shellfish in East Anglia, with crabs, mussels, whelks and white fish of the highest quality in abundance in local shops.

The distances involved in this area are not great. It is possible to make a base in King's Lynn, or any other stop along the coast, and explore from there. Personally, I would prefer to break up the journey by staying in Lynn for part and then in the more characterful eastern end of the coast for the remainder of the journey. Lynn is easily explored in a day; the coast can occupy a day's brisk car ride, with few excursions on foot, or happily engage a week of more thorough explorations.

King's Lynn

The port of King's Lynn has been a regular destination for European merchant vessels since the 14th century. Lynn remains a busy maritime centre today, though it has declined somewhat in importance from its height, in the early 18th century, when the value of goods passing through its docks made it the fourth most prosperous port in Britain after London, Bristol and Newcastle. Today's attractions for the visitor largely stem from Lynn's historic maritime past. There are impressive port buildings on the older part of the quayside by the Ouse, the 15th-century town hall is memorable, and the town retains its famous civic treasures, including one of the best examples of medieval gold cups in the world. There is more to Lynn than monuments, however. It is a thriving, cheerful town of character, with bustling markets on Tuesday, Friday and Saturday, a respected annual arts festival and an arts centre based around the ancient Guildhall of St George which would be envied by any town of comparable size.

The Duke's Head Hotel in the vast square of Tuesday Market Place is a good place to begin to explore the town. In fact, there are markets here on Tuesdays and Fridays, a fact which should be taken into account when trying to park in central Lynn. The hotel is an imposing 17th-century construction which dominates the three-acre marketplace, the most impressive of the ancient buildings which line the sides of the square. Leave by the river side along King Street, lined with attractive 17th- and 18th-century frontages, many of them former merchant's homes. To the right, now converted into the theatre of the Fermoy Arts Centre is the Guildhall of St George, which is claimed to be the oldest example of a medieval merchant guildhall still preserved in Britain. Suggestions that Shakespeare once acted here should be taken with a pinch of salt, but it is certain that the hall had been used as a theatre long before the notion was revived in modern times.

The Ouse runs behind the line of King Street to the South Quay and is soon seen when one reaches the Custom House, built in 1683 in the Palladian style. This curious, foursquare building perched in solitary fashion close to the docks has long served as an emblem for the town. The view of this part of the town today must be little changed in substance from that which greeted the adventurous sailors of the 17th and 18th centuries. Lynn mariners manned many a dangerous voyage; George Vancouver sailed with Cook before charting the west coast of North

America and sailing round Vancouver Island at the end of the 18th century.

The quayside is still busy with trade, though the modern port container business looks elsewhere. As Lynn's fashionability grows, spurred by the prospect of a new fast rail link to London, several of the handsome quayside warehouses are being converted to luxury apartments, partly with the commuter trade in mind. Doubtless the garrulous sailors of centuries ago who caroused around this part of town would be somewhat bemused to find their old quarters occupied by long-distance London stockbrokers. But the change has benefited the area enormously, bringing new life to lovely old buildings which might otherwise have faced the demolition men. Off South Quay lies Thoresboy College, originally priests' homes from the early 16th century, now used as a youth hostel. Further along, in St Margaret's Lane, are warehouses from the 15th century which once belonged to the Hanseatic League, the trade syndicate based in Hamburg which dominated merchant shipping across the North Sea and beyond in the Middle Ages. Moving away from the river here leads to the irregular shape of the Saturday Market Place, with the 12th-century St Margaret's Church and the photogenic 15th-century town hall of the Guildhall of the Holy Trinity. The church is for the dedicated; the Guildhall is essential viewing, if only for its collection of the civic treasures of Lynn.

The treasures are seen in the vaulted undercroft of the town hall, entered through the tourist information office in the adjoining Old Gaol. Two of its best-known items are, inaccurately, linked with King John who, in 1216, lost his baggage in the Wash while crossing from Lynn to Newark. King John's lost treasure has been a local folktale for centuries and several expeditions have set out in unsuccessful pursuit of its fabled wealth. We can say with some certainty, however, that the King John Cup and King John's Sword, both seen in the Lynn treasures, had no connection with the monarch whatsoever, though this does nothing to detract from their beauty or value.

The cup is priceless, being the oldest medieval cup and cover known. It dates from the 14th century and is made from silver and enamel, gilded with scenes of hunting. No town, and certainly no museum, has anything similar. The sword is a ceremonial item made in 1529, carried by dint of the town's Royal Charter which allows the mayor to be preceded by a sword of state and four maces at arms in all civic processions. The Charter was given by Henry VIII; the ceremonial maces, made in 1711, are also on display.

Lynn's history has endowed it with a small mountain of charters, deeds

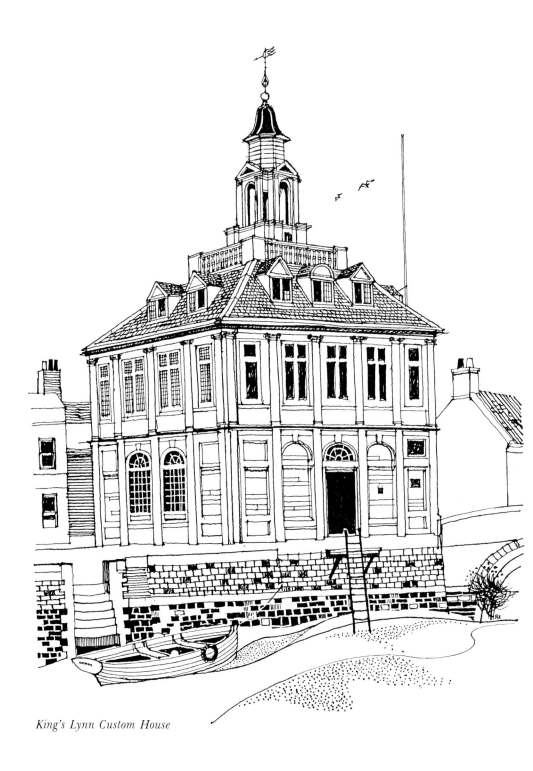

King's Lynn Custom House

and minute books which go back to the 12th century. Several are on display, telling tales of ancient Lynn lives great and small, from court records of minor misdemeanours to the letters patent granted by Henry VII which changed the borough's name from Bishop's Lynn to King's Lynn. This latter act was not simple generosity; Henry had seized the assets of the Bishop of Norwich which included rights to the borough of Lynn. The 'Red Register' on display records meetings of the mayor and councillors in the 14th century and is one of the oldest paper books in the world.

A short walk along Bridge Street, past more former merchantmen's homes, reveals the Greenland Fishery, built in 1605 as a private house but later an inn of some ill-repute used by men in the whaling trade, now used as offices. In London Road lies the original city gate for those entering from the south, while in Tower Gardens, off St James's Street, are the remains of a 15th-century tower once part of the Greyfriars monastery. The old town High Street runs from the Saturday Market Place back to the Tuesday Market where this walk began. It borders on the modern, unremarkable town centre shopping development which forms the outward face of Lynn to anyone who does not press on beyond the grey and featureless storefronts.

The north Norfolk Coast

King's Lynn stands at the periphery of East Anglia. To the west and north lies Lincolnshire, running flat and featureless to the Humber. The main coast road leading from Lynn along the north Norfolk coastline is full of interest as far as Cromer and one of the most pleasing drives to be had in the whole of East Anglia.

The small village of Castle Rising, four miles from Lynn, was once a rival port until the coastline receded taking trade with it. One can gain a measure of its past importance from the magnificent castle set on its own defensive embankment. Castle Rising is an ornate fortified keep, reached through a gatehouse guarding the bridge which leads to the embankment. Parts of the roof have disappeared, but the interior, with its great hall and stone stairs, remains impressive. English Heritage organise musical and historical pageants from time to time, though the castle is equally enjoyable off season.

Castle Rising was probably built on the site of Roman fortifications and has seen visits by several English monarchs. One was Queen Isabella 'the

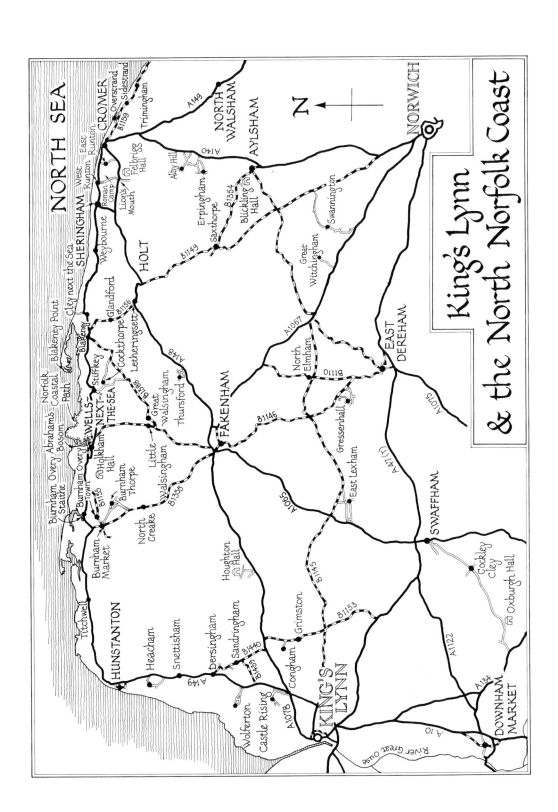

she-wolf of France', who conspired with her lover Roger Mortimer in the imprisonment and murder of her husband, the hapless Edward II. Her punishment, by her son Edward III, was confinement to Castle Rising for 27 years, apparently in some splendour. The village itself is pretty with several Tudor buildings and a Norman church largely rebuilt.

A magnet for modern royalty lies three miles north, the Sandringham estate which has been in the hands of the Royal Family since it was bought in 1861 by the then Prince of Wales, later Edward VII. Sandringham is the private property of the Queen, not an official residence supported by the public purse. Nevertheless, the grounds and house are open to the public when the Queen or any member of the Royal Family is not in residence. There is a nature trail and picnic areas and anyone may visit or worship at the estate's church. The Victorian house is of interest mainly as a curiosity. This is very much a private home for the Royal Family, who worship in the estate church and, when in residence, take part in local life as normally as security and protocol allow. The Sandringham Flower Show held in July is always a high point of the year.

In summer, the air around Heacham, a few miles north, announces the local floral industry. This is the lavender capital of England, with field after fragrant field under cultivation. An enormous variety of species, not all of them lavender in colour, can be seen and bought, and there is a wide selection of lavender-based soaps and perfumes made locally.

Hunstanton

The first large town after leaving King's Lynn, Hunstanton is somewhat atypical of the area since it resembles little more than a pleasant, conventional English seaside resort with little to set it apart from scores of others in the land. The town is divided into two parts, old and new, though there is little to distinguish them to the eye. The amusement arcades have a muted presence, but it is impossible to pretend that Hunstanton can compare in interest with any of its near neighbours to the east. The beach is unsurpassed, however, clean and sandy, and there are clifftop walks which give good views across the Wash to Boston Stump. Boating is a popular pastime and there is a splendid modern innovation for those who have never outgrown the habit of poking around seaside rock pools looking for the darting movements of small fish. The Hunstanton Sea Life Centre is a sophisticated aquarium complex which houses a marvellous collection of seafish large and small, local and exotic, presented to the public with admiration and enthusiasm. Oh, and realism too... since the exhibition will also remind you that the annual per capita consumption of fish fingers in Britain is 26, and if they were placed end to end they would stretch around the world three times.

The Burnhams

Past Hunstanton we start to enter a more individual part of Norfolk, where there is little in the way of mass development and many villages remain as unspoilt today as they were a century ago. This is also the territory of the 'twitcher', bird spotters supreme who can be seen lurking in the strangest spots, cars drawn hastily to a halt, a large pair of binoculars clasped tightly to the face. The northern coast is a Mecca for bird-watchers who will travel hundreds of miles for a brief sighting of some rarity announced on the twitcher's grapevine. The dedication and skill with which this level of bird-watching is pursued are difficult to describe or explain to anyone who has not seen the devoted twitcher stand in freezing rain for hours on end for a few seconds glance of a rare wader. But don't be put off if your interest is confined to a quick walk in the hope of spotting a flurry of unrecognisable but unusual feathers. The twitching crowd are full of advice and enlightenment for mere mortals so long as we don't blunder into their hides with radios blaring and a vocal Labrador on the loose. At Titchwell there is an RSPB reserve where waders and wildfowl dot around reed beds, salt marshland and sandy shores.

The Burnhams are a group of good-natured villages bearing the same prefix and casual rural charm. The largest is Burnham Market, the prettiest Burnham Overy but the little harbour at Burnham Overy Staithe is also worth a visit. Horatio Nelson, Norfolk's most famous mariner, was born in Burnham Thorpe in 1758, the son of the local rector. The old parsonage where he lived has since been demolished, but there are mementoes of Nelson in the village church and an admirable village pub, now the Lord Nelson, naturally. Another pub, the Captain Sir William Hoste in Burnham Market, is where Nelson supposedly collected his weekly newspapers from the Norwich Coach during the five years when the Admiralty was reluctant to give him a commission. The local folklore has it that Nelson took them to Overy Bank, by the Overy Staithe harbour, to read them, so keen was he to be close to his beloved sea. Much of the Burnhams would still be recognisable to Nelson. In these quiet little villages it is rather hard to imagine the quirks of fate which would uproot a boy of 13 from a north Norfolk parsonage to service in the West Indies, the

North Atlantic and the Mediterranean and finally a hero's death at Trafalgar in 1805 and a state funeral at St Paul's Cathedral the following January.

Travelling west one reaches Holkham Hall, Norfolk home of the Earls of Leicester and a Palladian country mansion of more engaging interest than the Royal residence of Sandringham. Holkham, as already noted, was the home of Coke of Norfolk, the 18th-century agriculturist who revolutionised British arable farming through the introduction of the system of four-course rotation. The 18th-century Italianate house has a lavish collection of tapestries and paintings while the grounds include a six-acre walled garden built in the 1780s.

Wells-next-the-Sea

The population of Wells can quadruple during the summer holidays but since, at best, it only amounts to some 2,500 people one need hardly fear the crowds. Wells is a charming spot, with a small harbour set behind bleak salt marshes and, away from the waterfront, quiet streets of Georgian houses. Whelk and skate boats still make occasional forays from Wells but the bulk of the trade lies in fertiliser and animal foodstuffs. There are several interesting restaurants and, in the Crown, a fine privately run former coaching inn with accommodation and a good dining room.

Sailing, walking and bird-watching are the three principal pastimes of Wells, while the more energetic can learn to windsurf. The beach is a mile from town, reached by a road or footpath leading from the west end of the harbour, and is vast at low tide, backed by sand dunes. Abraham's Bosom, once a safe haven for ships seeking shelter, has been cut off by the sea and turned into a boating lake. The Norfolk Coastal Path leaves the town at the east end of the quay and winds towards Stiffkey, an attractive route which can be as long as the walker chooses.

There is an obvious inland excursion from Wells to Walsingham and an opportunity to abandon the motor car. A small steam railway makes the eight-mile journey daily from April to September on the longest 10.25 inch gauge railway in Britain. The route was originally part of the Great Eastern Railway and runs through attractive countryside.

45

Walsingham

In a different world, Walsingham might today have been a sizable focus of Christian pilgrimage to rival Canterbury or Lourdes. The cult of Our Lady of Walsingham was, at one time, as devoutly followed as that of Thomas Becket or St James in Spain. It began around 1061 when one Lady Richoldis de Favarches saw a vision of the house at Nazareth where the Virgin was told of the impending holy birth by the angel Gabriel. Thus moved, the lady began to build a wooden copy of the house she saw. This was later miraculously moved to a new site a few yards to the west, and here the cult took root, with the appointment, in 1163, of the Augustinian Order to take control of the shrine and build a priory. Pilgrimage was both a religious and a commercial business in the Middle Ages, as Chaucer's tales expose so well. Stories of faith healing at the wooden shrine, the promise of seeing venerated relics of martyred saints – invariably bogus – brought thousands of visitors to Walsingham each year. So popular was the shrine that it changed the face of Norfolk, with the construction of religious hostelries along the principal pilgrim routes.

English monarchs were regular visitors to the shrine. Erasmus, encountered in Cambridge, wrote an account of his pilgrimage in 1511. All this came to an end during the reign of Henry VIII, though he had earlier visited Walsingham as a pilgrim. The dissolution of the monasteries saw the surrender of their properties to the Crown and the abbey fell into ruin. The much venerated shrine disappeared though recent excavations have shown that it was situated on the north side of the church. One contemporary account says that Henry, on his deathbed, bequeathed his soul to Our Lady of Walsingham.

In 1921 the cult of Our Lady of Walsingham was revived and now attracts Anglican and Roman Catholic pilgrims from all over the world. In

Walsingham, Norfolk

recent years it has also drawn the attention of groups of fundamentalist Christians who regard the cult of the Virgin as blasphemy and have heckled pilgrimage processions, a strange and depressing sight in the quiet medieval streets of Walsingham.

Confusingly, modern Walsingham is divided into two parts, Little and Great, the former being the larger. The village – one may consider both parts as a whole – is essentially medieval and picturesque from almost every angle. In the central Common Place stands a 400-year-old pump, the local museum and preserved courthouse and the tourist information centre. The Abbey Grounds are entered from the High Street. A footpath leads to the River Stiffkey, crossed by an ancient pack bridge on what was once the old road to Norwich. Close by lie the two wells which form an important part of the Walsingham legend since it was here that the wooden replica of the holy house was originally built before its miraculous move. The Queen Anne Abbey House now stands on part of the abbey, but there are interesting remains of the original construction.

The Anglican shrine of Our Lady of Walsingham, on Holt Road, was built in the 1930s and is Italianate, unlike anything else in Walsingham. It contains a modern statue of Our Lady of Walsingham made from the image on the seal of the medieval priory. The Roman Catholic shrine is the 14th-century Slipper Chapel on the road to Fakenham. This much restored chapel was the goal of a pilgrim's walk from Walsingham. The pilgrims walked barefoot – hence the chapel's name – and are said to have included Henry VIII. The journey is known as 'the Holy Mile' and is still followed by modern pilgrims. On the right, as you leave Walsingham, lie the ruins of a Franciscan friary founded in 1347.

Religion is the moving force behind modern Walsingham but there is nothing dour about the place. An afternoon excursion by train from Wells is an admirable way to tackle this English rarity – a modern pilgrim's village, and an interdenominational one at that.

Wells to Sheringham

After Wells, the coast road passes through the pretty village of Stiffkey and reaches, after seven miles, the small port of Blakeney, a happy little place of pleasure craft and fishing boats, flint buildings and bracing air. During the summer boats take visitors to Blakeney Point, an uninhabited spur of land across the Glaven estuary for bird-watching and views of the local seal population. There are long walks on largely unpopulated stretches of sandy beach.

Cley next the Sea is another former port that has been stranded by the receding sea, leaving behind a community of well-preserved flint cottages and an imposing church that seems out of proportion with Cley's present station in life. There is a small, working smokehouse, producing home-smoked kippers, bloaters, salmon and cods roe, and a fine pub with real ale and rooms, the George and Dragon. It was at the George, in 1926, that the Norfolk Naturalists Trust was formed, and a book of rare bird sightings is still maintained by the present owners, making the pub popular with visiting twitchers.

There is an obvious excursion inland from Blakeney or Cley to the small, largely Georgian town of Holt, but do not miss the stretch of road between Cley and Sheringham which passes through picturesque scenery. Holt is simply a pleasant and handsome country town, perhaps best known for Gresham's School which numbers Benjamin Britten and W. H. Auden among its former pupils. In Letheringsett, one mile west of Holt, there are walks and boats for hire in the four acres of Glavenside Gardens. The more mechanically minded may prefer the Muckleburgh Collection at Weybourne, a private display of tanks, armoured cars, guns and military vehicles from all over the world, many of them in alarmingly good working order.

Sheringham is a rather old-fashioned seaside resort with a small fishing fleet, a popular golf course, and a new venture designed to conquer the vagaries of the British climate, the 'Splash', an indoor family water centre with pools and amusements. At the heart of Sheringham remains a small, flint Norfolk fishing village, however. The tiny fleet continues to draw its boats up onto the pebble beach and there is strong traditional support for the local lifeboat. The North Norfolk Railway has preserved five miles of track from Sheringham to Holt via Weybourne, with steam services in historic rolling stock every Sunday from Easter to October and daily during August. Sheringham Park, acquired by the National Trust in 1987, is certainly worth a visit. It is regarded as one of the masterpiece's of the landscape gardener Humphrey Repton, who designed it in 1812. There is a drive of rhododendrons planted in the mid 19th century, magnificent in bloom each May, and a gazebo at the gardens' highest point offers outstanding views of the coastline.

The Norfolk Shire Horse Centre, at West Runton, two miles east of Sheringham on the way to Cromer, maintains a popular collection of shire and other working horses, and has a museum of horse-drawn farm equipment.

Cromer

The enchantment of Cromer is hard to define, but charming the place is nevertheless. Once again the outline of an old, flint-built fishing village can be discerned around the centre, dominated by the church tower of St Peter and St Paul, at 160 feet the tallest of any parish church in Norfolk. Most of the town is late Victorian or Edwardian, however. There is a splendid, well-preserved pier, opened in 1901, with good views of the old town. It stands on the site of an ancient town, Shipden Juxta Mare, which was swept into the sea by subsidence. In 1888 a pleasure steamer, The Victorian, was holed close to the present pier site, apparently by the remains of the spire of the Shipden church. To the east stands a curious octagonal lighthouse dating from 1833; in earlier times a beacon on the church tower had served as a warning to shipping.

The sea is still important to Cromer. Crab boats work daily except in the harshest of conditions, and there is little to rival the best of freshly boiled Cromer crab, available in any of the several good local fishmongers. The town's lifeboat has one of the most decorated histories of any in Britain. Henry Blogg, its cox from 1909 to 1947, won the RNLI's most coveted bravery award, the gold medal, no fewer than three times. There is a lifeboat museum in the Gangway while a terrace of fishermen's cottages near the parish church have been converted into an interesting town museum with one cottage refurnished to resemble a turn-of-the-century fisherman's home.

There are two superb National Trust properties within easy reach of the town. Felbrigg Hall dates from the 17th century and has original 18th-century furnishings, a walled garden, and an orangery with camelias. Blickling Hall, further south near Aylsham, is a dashing brick red Jacobean mansion with another fine garden. The estate has passed through many famous hands, among them King Harold and Sir John Fastolf – Shakespeare's Falstaff – and the grandfather of the unfortunate Anne Boleyn, one of Henry VIII's ill-fated wives.

Cromer is splendid walking country. There is a popular path over the cliffs to the east to the villages of Overstrand, two and a half miles away, and Sidestrand, one mile further. Continuing in this direction for five miles from Cromer brings the walker to Trimingham where the cliffs rise to 300 feet – mountains in East Anglian terms – and, on a clear day, the familiar spire of Norwich Cathedral, 20 miles away, is visible. There is another enjoyable walk west from Cromer to Sheringham, past the coastal villages of East Runton and West Runton, though the presence of caravan camps somewhat mars the views. West of Cromer, between the coastal road and the busy A148 to Fakenham, lies lovely wooded countryside. The oddly-named Lions Mouth, land close to Felbrigg Woods, is a popular local beauty spot, while at Roman Camp, just inland from West Runton, some 72 acres of countryside are now in the care of the National Trust. The Camp is the highest point in Norfolk, 330 feet above sea level, and a memorable place to end this exploration of the north Norfolk coast. Beyond Cromer, the coast is sparse and somewhat disappointing until it runs into the conventional holidaymaker's resort of Great Yarmouth, dealt with in the section on Norwich and the Norfolk Broads (see p. 95).

Castle Acre Priory, Swaffham, Norfolk

Tourist Information

The Old Gaol House
King's Lynn
Tel: 0553 763044
All year, Mon-Thur 10-5, Fri 10-4.30; May-
Oct also Sat 10-4. Regalia rooms and
exhibitions.

The Green
Hunstanton
Tel: 04853 2610
Oct-Apr, Mon-Fri 9-5.15; Apr-Sept, daily
9-5.45.

Wells Centre
Staithe Street
Wells-next-the-Sea
Tel: 0255 675542
Mar 20-Oct 31 ex Aug, daily 10-5; Aug daily,
10-6.

Red Lion House
Market Place
Fakenham
Tel: 0328 51981
Mar 20-Oct 31, daily 1-5.

Old Town Hall
Prince of Wales Road
Cromer
Tel: 0263 512497
Mar 20-Oct 31, daily 10-5.

Hotels

Tudor Rose
St Nicholas Street
King's Lynn
Tel: 0553 762824
Friendly hotel with good bar food and
restaurant – Cromer crab and vegetarian
dishes feature regularly.
Rooms: 18
Credit cards: Visa, Access
Rating ★★★

The Duke's Head
Market Place
King's Lynn
Tel: 0553 774996
Traditional, central hotel with a well-
respected dining room.
Rooms: 71
Credit cards: Access, Visa, Diners, Amex
Rating ★★★★

Knight's Hill Hotel
Knight's Hill Village
South Wootton
King's Lynn
Modernised farm complex on the outskirts
of the town, with good pub.
Rooms: 25
Credit cards: Access, Visa, Diners, Amex
Rating ★★★

Congham Hall
Grimston
King's Lynn
Tel: 0485 600250
Luxurious Georgian manor house on
40-acre estate. Heated pool.
Rooms: 11
Credit cards: Access, Visa, Diners, Amex
Rating ★★★★

The Old Rectory
Great Snoring
Fakenham
Tel: 0328 820597
Lovely country mansion dating from
around 1500 with Victorian additions.
Surrounded by walled garden of more than
an acre. Fine English food.
Rooms: 7
Credit cards: Diners, Amex
Rating ★★★★

Le Strange Arms
Golf Course Road
Old Hunstanton
Comfortable rooms close to sea and golf
course, one mile from town.

Le Strange Arms contd
Rooms: 30
Credit cards: Access, Visa, Diners, Amex
Rating ★★★

The Crown Hotel
The Buttlands
Wells-next-the-Sea
Tel: 0328 710209
Atmospheric privately-owned traditional
coaching inn with Tudor origins. Excellent
local food in restaurant and pub bar.
Rooms: 12
Credit cards: Access, Visa, Diners, Amex
Rating ★★★

Private Accommodation

The Manor House
Dersingham
King's Lynn
Tel: 0485 40228
Inexpensive farmhouse adjoining the
Sandringham estate. Home cooking with
local produce; stables available to guests
who wish to bring their own horses.
Rooms: 2
Credit cards: none
Rating ★★

The Hall
West Lexham
King's Lynn
Tel: 07605244/250
Georgian farmhouse 20 miles from the
coast. Trout fishing can be arranged; those
sufficiently experienced can use the family
horse and gig.
Rooms: 3
Credit cards: none
Rating ★★

Restaurants

See also hotels.
Lazybones
2 Brook Street
Cromer
Tel: 0263 515185

Wine-bar-style food in friendly atmosphere.
Closed Mondays and Tues/Wed evenings
Credit cards: Visa, Access
Rating ★★★

Food and Drink

Alby Crafts
Cromer Road
Erpingham
5m S Cromer
Tel: 0263 761590
Honey and honey products. Working bee
garden with observation hive.

Cley Smoke House
Cley next the Sea
Tel: Cley 740282
Local fish oak smoked on the premises.
Mail order available.

Congham Hall Herb Garden
Grimston
King's Lynn
Tel: Mrs C Foreman 0485 600250.
Potager and Herb Garden in country hotel,
with more than 200 different herbs. Tour
includes lunch and a talk on the use of
herbs.

Elmham Park Vineyards and Winery
Elmham House
North Elmham
6m S Fakenham
Tel: 036281 616
Producer of both grape and apple wine,
with good tour facilities. Summer evenings
groups only by appointment.

Lexham Hall Vineyard
East Lexham
King's Lynn
Tel: 0328 701288
Tour of vineyard and wine production
process. May-Oct, Mon-Fri by appointment
only.

Historic Houses

Sandringham House
8m NE King's Lynn
The Queen's country residence. Access to house and gardens, priced separately, with motor and dolls museums and nature trail. Mar 26-Sept 28, Mon-Thur 11-5, Sun 12-5. House closed Jul 17-Aug 5 incl. House and grounds closed Jul 21 - Aug 2 incl.

Oxburgh Hall
7m SW Swaffham
National Trust 15th-century moated house, collection includes needlework by Mary, Queen of Scots. Lovely and interesting gardens.
End of Mar, Apr-Oct, Sat and Sun 1.30-5.30, May 1-Sept 30, daily ex Thur and Fri, 1.30-5.30.

Houghton Hall
14m E King's Lynn
18th-century home of Robert Walpole now housing collection of around 20,000 model soldiers and other military artefacts. Mar 26-Sept 24, Thur, Sun and Bank Hols, gates open 12.30-5, house open 1-5.30.

Trinity Hospital
Castle Rising
5m NE King's Lynn
Chapel, dining hall and treasury of 17th-century almshouses. Apr-Sept, Tue, Thur, Sat 10-12, 2-6, closed at 4pm Oct-Mar.

Felbrigg Hall
3m SW Cromer
Immaculate 17th-century mansion now in the hands of the National Trust. Gardens, lake and woodlands.
Mar 25-Oct 29, 1.30-5.30, daily ex Tue and Fri. Gardens from 11am.

Holkham Hall
2m W Wells-next-the-Sea
Classical 18th-century mansion with fine collections of paintings – Van Dyke, Rubens, Poussin and Gainsborough – pottery and furniture. Six-acre walled garden. Mar 28-end Sept 1.30-5, ex Fri and Sat. Gardens all year, Mon-Sat 10-5, closed 1-2, Sun 2-5.

Blickling Hall
1m NW Aylsham
National Trust Jacobean home with fine furnishings, gardens and orangery. Mar 25-Oct 29 1-5, closed Mon and Thur. Garden 12-5.

Gardens

Glavenside Gardens
Letheringsett
1m W Holt
Water, rock and rose gardens in four acres with working water mill. All year, 10-sunset.

Kelling Park Hotel and Aviaries
Weybourne Road
Holt
Water gardens, pets corner, and exotic bird collection in six acres. April-Dec, Sun 12-5 or dusk if earlier, also Jun-Aug, Wed-Fri 11-6.

Norfolk Lavender
Caley Mill
Heacham
2m S Hunstanton
Working lavender farm with ornamental gardens. Lavender distillery working mid Jul-mid Aug. Daily all year, 10-5.30.

Mannington Hall Gardens
nr Saxthorpe
5m S Cromer
Large estate with lake, moat and woodland walks, important rose collection. April-Dec, Sun 12-5 or dusk; Jun-Aug, Wed-Fri 11-6. Annual rose festival in June.

The Pleasaunce
Overstrand
Cromer

The Pleasaunce contd
Ornamental gardens designed by Lutyens, off the Cromer to Mundesley road. End May-end Oct, Mon, Wed, Thur 2-5.

Sheringham Park
Sheringham
A148 Cromer to Holt
Woodland and formal gardens with spectacular views of the coast. Open all year, sunrise to sunset.

Swannington Manor Gardens
Swannington
9m NW Norwich
Magnificent old private gardens with orchid house and licensed restaurant. End Mar-end Sept, Wed and Bank Hol Mons 11-6.

Ancient Monuments

Castle Acre Priory
Swaffham
Ruined priory dating from the 11th century. EH. Mar-Sept, daily 10-6; winter, daily ex. Mon 10-4.

Castle Rising
Castle Rising
2m NE King's Lynn
Spectacular fortifications, once the seat of the Dukes of Norfolk. EH. Mar-Sept, daily 10-6. Winter, daily ex. Mon, 10-4.

Iceni Village and Museum
Cockley Cley
3m SW Swaffham
Reconstructed Iceni settlement with folk museum, nature trail and agricultural museum. Good for children. Mar-Oct, daily 1.30-5.30, mid Jul-mid Sept, daily 11.30-5.30.

Walsingham Abbey Grounds
Walsingham
5m N Fakenham
Original site of the shrine to Our Lady of Walsingham, remains of Augustinian priory.

Museums

Alby Lace Museum
Alby Craft Centre
5m S Cromer
Demonstrations of lacemaking techniques and a shop dedicated to lace. Mid Mar-mid Dec, Tue-Fri and Sun 10-5.

Cockthorpe Hall Toy Museum
Cockthorpe
Toys from Victorian times to the mid 1960s in 16th-century house. End Mar-end Oct, daily 10-5.30; winter, Mon-Fri 2-5, Sat and Sun 10-5.

Cromer Museum
East Cottages
Tucker Street
Cromer
Conventional local museum in Victorian fishermen's cottages. Mon 10-1, 2-5; Tue-Sat 10-5; Sun 2-5.

Museum of Gas and Local History
Fakenham
Tel: 0328 51696
The town's Victorian gasworks preserved with working engines. And a local museum. Apr-Oct, Thurs and Sun 2-5. Other times by appointment.

Glandford Shell Museum
Glandford
3m NW Holt
Shell collection from the local coast and beyond, some engraved. Jan-Feb, Mon-Thur 9.30-12.30; Mar-Nov, Mon-Thur 9.30-12.30, 2.30-4.30, Fri and Sat 2.30-4.30.

Norfolk Rural Life Museum
Gressenhall
2m NW East Dereham
Life in the rural Norfolk of old – housed in a former workhouse. Mar-Oct, Tue-Sat 10-5, Sun 2-5.30.

Bygones at Holkham
Holkham Park
Wells-next-the-Sea
Somewhat eccentric collection of fire
engines, cars and sundry Victorian
mechanical objects next to Holkham Hall.
May-Sept, Sun-Thur 1.30-5, also May and
Aug 11.30-5.

Lynn Museum
King's Lynn
Standard local museum. Mon-Sat 10-5.

Museum of Social History
27 King Street
King's Lynn
Social record of King's Lynn life over the
centuries – brass rubbing. Tue-Sat 10-5.

Regalia Rooms
Trinity Guildhall
King's Lynn
Tel: 0553 763044 .
Town treasury, including Royal charters and
the cup allegedly belonging to King John.
Telephone for details of opening times.

The Forge Museum
North Creake
3m S Burnham Market
Working traditional forge, one of the few
left in Norfolk. May-Sept, daily 12-5.

The Thursford Collection
Thursford
6m NE Fakenham
Unsurpassed collection of steam-driven
road locomotives and organs. Daily Mar
11-5, Apr 1-5, May 1-5, Jun-early Sept 11-5,
Sept-Oct 1-5, Oct 2-5. Closed Nov-mid Mar.
Wurlitzer concerts every Tues at 8pm from
mid June-end Sept.

Wolferton Station Museum
Wolferton
6m NE King's Lynn
Tel: 0485 40674.

Collection of Edwardian Royal travel
artefacts. By appointment.

Wildlife Parks and Reserves

Blakeney Point
nr Wells-next-the-Sea
Spit of National Trust land reached by boat
from Morston or Blakeney. Seals, birds,
observation hides. All year.

Cley Visitor Centre
Cley Marshes
Views of the Cley Marshes reserve, visited by
migrant bird colonies, displays and permits
for visiting reserve. Apr-Oct, Tue-Sun 10-5.

Snettisham
5m N King's Lynn
Wildfowl and waders on Wash gravel pits,
access from beach daily.

**Badley Moor Fish, Bird and Butterfly
Centre**
Badley Moor
East Dereham
Display of British and tropical butterflies
and water gardens. Mar-Oct, daily 10-5.

Kelling Park Aviaries
Weybourne Road
Holt
Tropical birds and wildfowl in six acres.
Daily 10-dusk.

Pensthorpe Waterfowl Park
Pensthorpe
Fakenham
Wildfowl collection, nature trails. Mar-Oct,
daily 11-5, Nov-Dec, weekends only.

Walks

Sandringham
7m NE King's Lynn
Nature trail through wood and heathland
of the Queen's estate. Two routes – $1\frac{1}{2}$ and
$2\frac{1}{2}$ miles.

Holt Lowes
1m S Holt
Well-organised woodland and heath walks
through more than 200 acres with parking
and toilets.

Other Diversions

Surf 55
55 St James's Street
King's Lynn
Tel: 0553 764356
Windsurfing school for the hardy.

Ilex House
Bases Lane
Wells-next-the-Sea
Tel: 0328 710556
Birdwatching courses.

Norfolk Cycling Holidays
Sandy Way
Ingoldisthorpe
King's Lynn
Tel: 0485 40642
Organised cycling breaks with
accommodation.

West Lexham Holidays
Old Post Office
West Lexham
King's Lynn
Tel: 07605 253
Hire of horse drawn caravans.

Pakenham Watermill

3 Inland Suffolk

The countryside and small villages and towns of mid and west Suffolk conjure up a picture of idyllic, rural and provincial England, an area of handsome towns and verdant fields. Bury St Edmunds is an ancient market town which has escaped the modern redevelopment which has marred many of its neighbours. Lavenham is an exquisite medieval wool town of half-timbered buildings, with two famous hotel/restaurants and an imposing Perpendicular church. Sudbury was the home of Gainsborough; his birthplace has been preserved and now houses an exhibition of his work. Bury or Lavenham are obvious and popular places to stay in the neighbourhood, and there are short and easy excursions to two other interesting villages, Clare and Long Melford. There are well-organised walks throughout the area, particularly in the Gipping valley, with its 17-mile country footpath from Stowmarket to Ipswich. This area can be sensibly combined with Constable Country by following the road from Sudbury along the Stour valley to Dedham (see p. 103). Inland Suffolk is also an easy addition to a visit to the Cambridge area (see p. 18). There is little need to choose two different bases here; a hotel in Lavenham or Bury is little more than a leisurely hour from any of the local sights.

Bury St Edmunds

The engaging market town of Bury St Edmunds must count as one of the most pleasant of East Anglia's urban communities. Modern redevelopment

Bury St. Edmunds — gateway

has been contained and, in important areas, almost completely halted. Bury is both delightful to look at and experience, a happy place of fine streets, interesting little shops and a fair smattering of sights. The Angel Hotel, itself one of the town's historic buildings, is an excellent base with rather more to do in the evenings than may be found in Lavenham.

Bury is named after St Edmund, the unfortunate boy king of East Anglia who was martyred by the Danes in AD 869 and, for a time, became the object of a national pilgrimage to his tomb in the town. Edmund, though from Saxony, succeeded Offa to the East Anglian throne at the age of 15. During one of the constant Danish incursions into the north of the kingdom, Edmund was captured and beheaded. Early martyrdom always becomes a king's reputation, and it may be that, in the fullness of time, Edmund could have won for himself an altogether different name. One need only recall Henry VIII, lauded as Defender of the Faith by the Pope when young, an outlaw of Rome and effective murderer of two of his wives when older, to see how history can shift its perspective in the lifetime of any monarch.

For a while, Edmund was seen as a hero of national resistance. His body was buried in Bury 30 years after his death, and a shrine built in his honour on the site of the present abbey ruins. Bury's standing was further improved by another monarch of dubious historic repute, King Canute who changed Edmunds Bury to the present Bury St Edmunds and gave endowments to the shrine of the martyr. Canute is popularly remembered as the fool who sat on a throne in the face of an incoming tide, ordering it to turn back. The story is misread; in truth he was a sensible and compromising monarch, in the original version of the tale he was trying to impress upon his courtiers the point that even he could not turn back the tide.

The Norman invasion, only 31 years after Canute's death, led to the construction of the abbey alongside the River Lark and its tributary, the Linnet, incorporating Edmund's shrine into the new church. In 1214, the town was once more at the centre of English history when 25 of the most powerful barons of the nation met in the church and agreed to force King John to accept the Magna Carta, signed at Runnymede in the following year.

Any exploration of Bury should begin in Angel Hill, only a matter of yards from the scene of these historic events. This was the former entrance to the abbey complex, a meeting place for the bands of travelling monks, hucksters and the genuinely devout who formed the hub of medieval pilgrimage. Two of the five original gates into the abbey remain, the 14th-century Abbey Gate and the earlier Norman Tower. They lead into the abbey grounds, now a pleasant municipal park in which the design of the original religious community can still be discerned, though quite what a medieval traveller would have made of the modern bowling green and tennis courts one can only conjecture. There is little to show that this was a scene of pious pilgrimage a century before Canterbury. Next to the Norman Tower stands St Edmundsbury Cathedral, a modernised medieval church promoted to cathedral status in 1913. Further south, St Mary's Church, just outside the old abbey walls, has a fine angel and wagon roof, the tomb of Henry VIII's sister, Mary Tudor, and a lovely churchyard.

Also in Angel Hill, but on the other side from the abbey, can be found several lovely old buildings: the Angel Hotel, with its 13th-century undercroft, and the Georgian Athenaeum, where Dickens gave readings are just two. The Gershom Parkington Collection of Clocks and Watches, in a Queen Anne house on the corner of the hill, maintains a comprehensive display of timepieces ancient and modern. At the foot of Crown Street is the Regency Theatre Royal, designed by William Wilkins who is best known for the National Gallery in London.

The commercial centre of medieval Bury lay a little to the east, around Cornhill and the Butter Market. Here is preserved one of the oldest stone houses in the country, Moyses Hall, somewhat restored by the Victorians, now housing the lively borough museum. South from Cornhill lie interesting and attractive streets of varying antiquity, many of them apparently Georgian but in fact of earlier origin refaced in the late 18th and early 19th centuries. The Corn Exchange is a grand Victorian monument to the industry which has been Bury's principle source of income over the centuries. Its fate may give a clue to why modern day Bury remains so delightful. In the late 1950s, developers lodged plans to demolish the building. Such a public outcry ensued that the idea was dropped almost instantly, all this at a time when most of the town's neighbours were busily dismantling their medieval heritage. Bury is a place of admirable character, for which we should all be grateful.

The most accessible country house is Ickworth, two miles south, a National Trust property with an extraordinary oval house, art and silver collections, a formal garden and walks in parkland where deer can be watched from hides.

Lavenham

The lovely timbered streets of Lavenham represent a picture postcard image of rural medieval England. Lavenham has few rivals for the title of loveliest village of its kind in the country. It would be unthinkable to visit this part of Suffolk without including it on the itinerary; the village is one of the principal sights of East Anglia and almost entirely unspoilt.

Although to modern eyes, Lavenham, in the rolling countryside south of Bury, is an idyllic agricultural village, in fact, nothing could be further from the truth. It would be more accurate to classify the place as a medieval industrial town, the equivalent of Birmingham or Manchester rather than some bucolic community of farm labourers. Lavenham flourished on industry and commerce, not the produce of its agricultural estates. During the reign of Henry VIII, it was ranked the 14th most wealthy town in England, principally on the manufacture of cloth. When the wool trade failed elsewhere, Lavenham began to specialise in

Lavenham, Suffolk

horsehair and coconut matting, trades that flourished in the village until early this century.

Today, tourism is the principal industry, but Lavenham has resisted the temptation to flaunt its charms and remains a quiet, stately yet local village of considerable innate charm. On a purely indulgent note, it should also be said that the village possesses the rare English equivalent of a fine French provincial hotel and restaurant, one run entirely, it should be said, by a French staff.

There is a simple circular walk which will encompass all the principal sights of Lavenham in half a day. Begin in the Market Place which lies just off the main High Street on the main Hadleigh to Bury St Edmunds road. Here stand several historic buildings, among them the Great House, once the home of the poet Stephen Spender, now unquestionably the best place to stay and eat in the village. The Corpus Christi Guildhall is Lavenham's most famous building, the 16th-century meeting hall of one of the village guilds and one of the best preserved timber-framed buildings of its period in the country. It is now in the hands of the National Trust and houses a small local museum, though the real point of interest in entering is to see this architectural wonder from the inside, with its skeleton timber frame laid bare to reveal the standard form of construction of medieval middle to upper class housing. Little Hall, next to the Great House, is a former medieval house which now acts as the headquarters of the ever vigilant Suffolk Preservation Society. It is open by appointment and on Saturday and Sunday afternoon in the summer. The Great House itself, while Georgian in appearance, is, in reality, a refaced timber building of similar medieval origins, as anyone staying there will soon appreciate.

Turn down Barn Street, by the Little Hall, to find, on the right, another timbered merchant's home, Molet House, then follow Bolton Street into Shilling Street which runs downhill to Water Street. Shilling Street, which is not obviously found by idle wandering, is one of the most picturesque in the village, with a variety of old houses of individual character, as photogenic as more famous thoroughfares of its kind, such as Rye's Mermaid Hill and Shaftesbury's Gold Hill (though, unlike them, not cobbled).

At the foot of the hill turn right, past more old cottages. In Barn Street, to the right, stands the former Grammar School which numbered the young Constable among its pupils (he was bitterly unhappy there). Returning to Water Street once more, we reach the distinctly crooked timbered De Vere House. Fears for its safety should be allayed; the building was virtually rebuilt in its present state in the 1920s. A little way along is the Priory, a large private house open daily during the summer from 10.30am to 5.30pm. The Priory is an excellent example of private restoration of an ancient monument. The site has served as a Benedictine priory and the home of a local clothing family, but it was almost beyond repair until rescued privately by the Casey family. The timber-framed house has been restored and homemade teas and lunches are served in the refectory. There is a herb garden and a gift shop selling tapestries and other unusual items.

Almost opposite stands Lady Street, leading back to the Market Place. At the foot of the hill are several impressive Tudor buildings and the Wool Hall, another timber-framed guildhall. Returning to Water Street brings us to the Swan, a wonderful, sprawling timbered inn which would be even more enjoyable were it owned and run by an individual proprietor instead of the faceless Trust House Forte.

Turn left and begin to climb the southern hill of the village towards the great church of St Peter and St Paul, passing yet more handsome old houses on the way. If you are beginning to wonder whether Lavenham possesses any unbecoming homes, then look to the right where a hideous squat estate of modern bungalows has been allowed to clothe the side of the hill nearest the village. The church of Lavenham is an abiding image of the village, a Perpendicular giant built on the donations of rich local clothiers from 1485 to 1525, though the chancel survives from its Norman predecessor. One of the fund-raising events organised at the time was a hunt, run by the Lord of Manor, John de Vere, the 13th Earl of Oxford, which contrasts nicely with the village tea parties of today. The interior tends to come as something of a disappointment; there was substantial 'restoration' by both Puritans and Victorians which removed many of the earlier features.

Do not, as most unguided visitors do, now return to the village the way you came, for there is a delightful little walk around the back of the church. The farmhouse here stands on the site of the de Vere's former manor. A footpath leads from the churchyard, through Saffron Garden, past the lake known, somewhat misleadingly, as the Fishpond and into Hall Lane. From here, turn right to rejoin the High Street which, with yet more fine old shops and homes, provides a suitable return route to the Market Place.

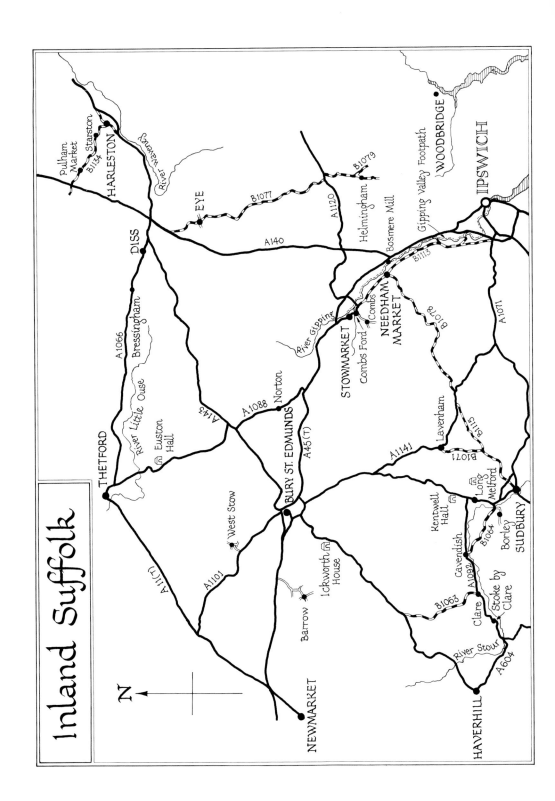

Inland Suffolk

Long Melford, Clare and Sudbury

South of Lavenham lie three small and ancient towns which combine into a delightful day's excursion. Long Melford lies on the main Sudbury to Bury road, an extended town of medieval beauty and a vast village green overlooked by Melford Hall, a turreted Tudor mansion now in the hands of the National Trust. The hall has a marvellous banqueting hall and formal garden, largely unchanged since Tudor times. Astonishingly, another great country house lies only a little way along the road to Bury, Kentwell Hall, Tudor with later additions and a colourful history. Kentwell was slighted – reduced to rubble as a punishment – after the Civil War, burnt out in Victorian times and is now restored privately. It can easily occupy a day for the family. In addition to the moated house, there is a rare farm animal collection, costume displays, catering facilities and a range of special events which vary from open air Shakespeare to recreations of Tudor domestic life.

It is worth walking down the length of the village, from the green to the 18th-century ford bridge where the old main street begins. There is a profusion of handsome old houses and the Bull, an old coaching inn, is a pleasant spot for lunch.

Turn west at Long Melford for Clare. On the way is the little village of Cavendish, one of those happily located thatched communities that forever finds its way into country calendars. Clare is a lovely little town with another imposing wool church and a collection of grand houses that veer from half-timbered to Georgian elegance. This was once a busy and important town of commerce, as the remains of the Norman castle and Augustinian friary, the latter now a wild garden open daily to the public for free, indicate. A pleasant country park has now been established on the site of the castle, with a nature trail, butterfly garden and waterfowl area in 25 acres, it is one of the best in Suffolk.

Return to Cavendish and follow the road to Sudbury, a lively market town on the Suffolk side of the Stour, which marks the border with Essex. A brief detour for curiosity's sake alone could be made to Borley, only a few decades ago infamous for its rectory, known in psychic circles as 'the most haunted house in Britain'. The renowned rectory is no more; it burnt down mysteriously some years ago. Nor do villagers take kindly to Borley's reputation, since for most folk it seems to be just a pleasant country village with a pretty location.

Sudbury is best known as the home town of Gainsborough. Here the market town of old has been modernised, not as brusquely as some of its neighbours but visibly nevertheless. One gets a very clear hint of what Bury and Lavenham have fortunately escaped. The artist's house, at the foot of Market Hill, is certainly worth a visit, the only birthplace of a major British artist currently open to the public. Gainsborough was born here in 1727 and lived in Sudbury until he went to study in London at the age of 13. He returned to the little town briefly, later settling in Ipswich. The house contains more works by Gainsborough than any other gallery, among them many portraits from his Suffolk period. There is also a collection of personal effects and, in the summer, a display of modern architecture.

The Gipping Valley

East of Bury lies Stowmarket, an unpretentious modern agricultural and industrial town notable for little except the Museum of East Anglian Life, with its permanent displays and regular special events such as traction engine rallies and sheepshearing displays. However, the local authority, perhaps aware that the area is left somewhat wanting by the historic splendours of its neighbours to the west, has a commendable record for countryside amenities. There is a first rate picnic site close to Stowmarket town centre. Church Meadow, a little over a mile south near Combs Ford, offers good countryside views. Combs Ford itself is a quiet spot for walking and there is picnic and play equipment here too. Needham Lake, near Needham Market, is a superbly managed environmental project, with wildfowl, a nature reserve, picnic sites and walks alongside the lake and the River Gipping. The

The Gipping Valley

66

Gipping Valley Footpath, which runs from Stowmarket to Ipswich, passes here, and nearby Bosmere Mill is a good place for a pub lunch.

Tourist Information

6 Angel Hill
Bury St Edmunds
Tel: 0284 763233.
Nov-Mar, Mon-Fri 9-5 and Sat 10-12; Apr-
Oct, Mon-Thur 9-5.30, Fri 9-5, Sat 10-4.30,
also Jul and Aug, Sun 10-12.

Wilkes Way
Stowmarket
Tel: 0449 676800
Easter-Dec, Mon-Fri 9-5.30, Sat 9-4.30; Jan-
Mar, Mon-Fri 9.30-5.30, Sat 10-2.

The Guildhall
Market Place
Lavenham
Tel: 0787 248207
Easter-end Oct, 10-4.45.

Hotels

The Swan
High Street
Lavenham
Tel: 0787 247431
The 14th-century Swan is one of
Lavenham's largest medieval buildings and
retains its character in spite of the
international style of management. THF.
First-class restaurant, but distinctly over-
priced.
Rooms: 48
Credit cards: Access, Visa, Diners, Amex
Rating ★★★★

The Great House
Market Place
Lavenham
Tel: 0787 247431
Justly famous 15th-century house, once the
home of the poet Stephen Spender. Now
French-run with the atmosphere of a high
class provincial French hotel. Tables in the
pretty courtyard in summer. Superb
restaurant serving classic French dishes with
fixed price and a la carte menus. Closed for
part of January.
Rooms: 4 suites
Credit cards: Access, Visa, Diners, Amex
Rating ★★★★

The Angel Hotel
3 Angel Hill
Bury St Edmunds
Tel: 0284 753926
Historic and atmospheric town centre hotel
dating from the 15th century. Dickens gave
two readings of *David Copperfield* at the
Angel. Excellent traditional dining room.
Rooms: 40
Credit cards: Access, Visa, Diners, Amex
Rating ★★★★

Corders Hotel
Bury Road
Lawshall
6m S Bury St Edmunds
Tel: 0284 830314
Quiet former farmhouse on two acres of
grounds.
Rooms: 8
Credit cards: Access, Visa, Diners, Amex
Rating ★★★

Private Accommodation

The Old Guildhall
Mill Street
Gislingham
Eye
Tel: 037 983361
Comfortable village rooms each with private
bath in an old house between the A143 and
A140.
Rooms: 3
Credit cards: none
Rating ★★

Lodge Farm
Bressingham
Diss
Tel: 037988 629
16th-century farmhouse accommodation,
rare sheep, horses and poultry on farm.

Also a cottage to sleep four for short let.
Rooms: 3
Credit cards: none
Rating ★★

Ounce House
Northgate Street
Bury St Edmund's
Tel: 0284 61779/755192
Large Victorian house with interesting
interior. Family-run by wife of a local
surveyor.
Rooms: 4
Credit cards: none
Rating ★★

Malting Farm
Blo Norton Road
South Lopham
Diss
Tel: 0379 88201
Elizabethan farmhouse on working dairy;
inglenooks and four-poster beds. No
smoking.
Rooms: 3
Credit cards: none
Rating ★★

Restaurants

See also hotels.

Golden Palace
19 Hatter Street
Bury St Edmunds
Tel: 0284 754331

Interesting Peking and Cantonese food a
cut above the usual Chinese restaurant fare.
Credit cards: Access, Visa
Rating ★★★

Food and Drink

Pulham Vineyards
Mill Lane
Pulham Market
Diss
Tel: 037 976 672

White table wine from Müller Thurgau and
Auxerrois vines. Tour of winery, cellars and
bottling plant. Open daily ex. Mon, by
appointment.

Boyton Vineyards
Hill Farm
Boyton End
Stoke-by-Clare
5m W Sudbury
Tel: 0440 61893
Wine tasting and vineyard trail. Entrance
fee. Open most weekends by appointment.

Cavendish Manor Vineyards
Nether Hall Manor
Cavendish
Sudbury
Tel: 0787 280221
Well organised tour with opportunity to
taste and buy. All year, daily 11-4.

Starston Fayre
Cranes Watering Farm Shop
Starston
Harleston
Tel: 0379 852387
Dairy products from herd of Jersey and
Guernsey cows. Cream, ice cream, yogurt
cheese, butter and lemon curd. Local
produce includes dairy-fed pork and corn-
fed poultry. Mon-Sat 10-6, Sun 10-12, 10-6
Jul and Aug. Tours on request, milking daily
4-6pm.

Aspall Cider
Cider House
Stowmarket
Tel: 0278 860510
Manufacturer of cider, apple juice and
vinegar. The press room, dating from 1728,
is open to the public. Mon-Fri 9-12.30, 1.30-
3.30.

Wheldons PYO
Sudbury
Tel: 0787 74322

Wheldons PYO contd

Pick-your-own soft fruit, plums and apples in season. Off A134 between Newton and Sudbury.

Historic Houses

Gainsborough's House
Sudbury
East Anglia's best known painter was born in this Georgian house which now has a permanent display of his work and that of contemporaries.
Mar 25- Sept 30, Tue-Sat 10-5, Sun 2-5; winter, Tue-Sat 10-4, Sun 2-4.

Ickworth
Horringer
3m SW Bury St Edmunds
National Trust Palladian mansion with famous rotunda. Furniture collections, park, garden and woodland. May 1-Sept 30, 9.30 daily ex Mon and Thur, house 1.30-5.30, park dawn-dusk.

Kentwell Hall
Long Melford
Sudbury
Tel: 0787 310207
Family-owned moated redbrick Tudor manor house with daily recreations of medieval life. Restoration from near ruin began in 1971. Rose maze and regular events, from maypole dancing to open-air theatre. Opening times vary.
Confirm by telephone.

Euston Hall
Euston
3m S Thetford
Paintings by Stubbs and Van Dyck, landscaping by Brown and others. The 18th-century house is the home of the Duke of Grafton, descendant of one of the sons of Charles II. Jun 1-Sept 28, Thur 2.30-5.30.

Guildhall
Lavenham
National Trust-run 16th-century timber-framed building with an exhibition of the history of Lavenham as a wool town.
Mar-25-Nov 4, daily 11-1, 2-5.30.

Little Hall
Lavenham
Tel: 0787 247179.
Built a century before the Guildhall, this former private house is run by the Suffolk Preservation Society, and has collections of furnishings and pictures. Mar 25-Oct 14, Sat, Sun and Bank Hols 2.30-6 or by appointment.

The Priory
Lavenham
Tel: 0787 247417.
Former priory and private home restored from ruin recently. Herb garden and stained glass displays in timber-framed medieval house. Easter-Oct 31, daily 10.30-5.30. Groups all year by appointment.

Gardens

Bressingham Gardens
Diss
One of the country's foremost suppliers of quality plants, and a regular prizewinner at the Chelsea Flower Show. Six acres of richly stocked beds. Steam railway with five miles of track and a museum of more than 50 engines.
End Apr-Sept, Sun and Bank Hol Mons, June-Sept, Thurs, Aug, Weds, 10-5.30.

Helmingham Hall Gardens
Helmingham
6m E Stowmarket
Tel: 047 339 363
Walled garden of moated private house (closed) with ancient roses and kitchen garden. Highland cattle and deer park. End Apr-Oct, Sun 2-6. Coaches Sun and Wed by appointment.

Ancient Monuments

Bury St Edmunds Abbey
Bury St Edmunds
Attractive gardens now cover the site of the abbey. Magnificent Norman tower, 14th-century abbey gate are the principal remains. Open daily.

West Stow Anglo-Saxon Village
West Stow Country Park
7m NW Bury St Edmunds
Reconstruction of Anglo-Saxon village. All year daily, 10-5. Phone to confirm visit: Alan Baxter, 2 Wideham Cottages, West Stow. Tel: 028 484 718.

Museums

Gershom Parkington Collection of Clocks and Watches
Angel Corner
Bury St Edmunds
Valuable collection of timepieces, some more than 400 years old. Mon-Sat 10-5, Sun 2-5.

Moyse's Hall Museum
Bury St Edmunds
Evidence from the Maria Marten Red Barn murder, local history and natural history. Mon-Sat 10-5, Sun 2-5.

Suffolk Regiment Museum
Gibraltar Barracks
Bury St Edmunds
Military items from the Suffolk and Cambridgeshire regiments. Mon-Fri 10-12, 2-4.

Museum of East Anglian Life
Stowmarket
Tel: 0449 612229
Private 30-acre 'open air museum' with a regular program of changing events. Working mill and smithy, wagon rides and cameos of rural life. March-Oct 11-5, Sun 12-5. Telephone for programme of events.

Wildlife Parks and Reserves

Norton Tropical Bird Gardens
7m E Bury St Edmunds
International collection of exotic birds covering four acres with tropical house. All year, daily 11-6 or dusk.

Tropical Butterflies
Barrow
5m W Bury St Edmunds
Rare butterfly collection, gardens and small steam railway. Mar-Oct, daily 10-5.

Walks

Walks along dismantled railway lines, varying in length up to four miles. Leaflet costs 20p from Suffolk County Council, County Hall, Ipswich.

Clare Castle
nr Sudbury
Nature trail around ruins of castle and former railway centre. Open daily.

Painters Way
Long distance – 24 miles – walk from Sudbury to Manningtree through picturesque countryside. Booklet 75p from Peddar Publications, Croft End, Bures, Suffolk CO8 5JN.

Aldeburgh Beach

4 The Suffolk Coast

The bleak coastline north of Ipswich has several small villages and towns that have attracted artists and writers for many years. The atmosphere is unlike anywhere else in East Anglia, remote, often windswept and unpretentious. The small town of Woodbridge on the River Deben is one of the more sophisticated communities, with hotels and restaurants serving weekend visitors from London. Further north, Orford, Aldeburgh and Southwold are more local in character. The area is a popular destination for bird-watchers interested in the wildlife of the region; herons and the rare avocet are among the species to be found. Snape Maltings, near Aldeburgh, is world famous as the home of the Britten-Pears music school and the annual Aldeburgh festival, started by the composer Benjamin Britten and the singer Peter Pears who lived in the area.

There are hotels and simpler bed and breakfast accommodation the length of the coast. They vary enormously in atmosphere, from open-fired seaside pubs to luxury, characterful hotels. A pleasant contrast can be made by dividing a visit into two, one part in the comfy, tourist-oriented surroundings of Woodbridge, the second in a more remote location, such as Southwold. While distances are relatively short, minor roads are often narrow and winding, and the main trunk road, the A12, is extremely busy. So there is also a practical reason for dividing the visit into two.

Woodbridge

Woodbridge lays claim to the title of the most attractive small town in Suffolk. Lavenham and a few others might wish to dispute this notion, but there can be no denying the charm of Woodbridge even if, in a sense, it is somewhat out of place.

Handsome, engaging, solidly mercantile in character and appearance, Woodbridge is a well-preserved 16th-century port and market town which has escaped most of the depradations of modern urban life – the motor car excepted. It is quite unlike the sprawling mass of Ipswich to the south and also totally unakin to the frugal and spartan pleasures of the coastal villages and small towns of the north, which is why I glance anxiously at the map whenever I pass through. Never mind. It is impossible not to like and admire the place, even if it does instil a tiny intuition of unreality.

This is serious yachting country. Landlubbers who do not know their rigs from their rudders may be hard pressed to hold an intelligent conversation in certain local hostelries. The pleasure sailors make the most of the safe Deben estuary all year long and do not fear to venture further. I have seen the name Woodbridge gracing craft harboured as far away as the eastern Mediterranean which shows that the modern amateur sailor is, in some cases, no less adventurous than his predecessors.

Woodbridge was an active and wealthy port for centuries. Ocean going cargo boats were built here and there was a busy trade in supplying them with locally made sailcloth and other provisions. The size of the trade is reflected in the modern town, for Woodbridge is blessed with an enormous collection of rich merchant's houses of Tudor, Jacobean and Georgian origins and a well-preserved quayside where weatherboarded mills stand happily by old mansions.

The quay is the most picturesque part of town and a natural magnet for visitors. The 18th-century timber-boarded tidemill on the quay has been preserved and contains working machinery. In the town, the most striking building is the Shire Hall on Market Hill, a grand Elizabethan municipal structure in red brick fronted by a double staircase. It was built by the town's principal benefactor, Thomas Seckford, whose home outside the town is now one of the area's smartest hotels. All around the hall are Tudor and Georgian homes and shops, and in New Street there is a 17th-century weighing machine used for weighing the loads of carts as they entered the town. One of the few remaining in the country, it was last used in 1880. Woodbridge Museum, on Market Hill, documents the town's maritime history and also the excavation of the Sutton Hoo burial ship, four miles away in Sutton, which revealed the ceremonial interment of a wealthy East Anglian noble of the sixth or seventh century AD. The Sutton Hoo treasures are now in the British Museum.

One of the best views of the town and the surrounding area is from the steeple of the parish church of St Mary, some 108 feet above ground. The Deben meanders towards the sea and the polyglot roofs of the old town betray their age. To the south is the National Trust parkland of Kyson Hill while north east lies Rendlesham Forest and the unique charm of the unspoilt Suffolk coast.

Orford and Butley

Beyond Woodbridge, driving towards the coast, there is a distinct change in atmosphere. The cosmopolitan bustle of Ipswich and Woodbridge soon disappear and the landscape becomes one of forest, marsh and heathland. Follow the Orford road, the B1084 through Butley; the coastal cul-de-sacs to Bawdsey and Hollesley are of little interest. There are walks in Rendlesham Forest signposted by the road.

Butley is now little more than a hamlet, though this was once the site of one of the most important religious communities in East Anglia, Butley Priory, founded in 1171. All that remains now is the grand gatehouse in which one can see the arms of England and France and the heraldic emblems of great East Anglian families. Butley is also known for its oysters, though their most famous outlet lies a few miles further east, at the coastal village of Orford.

The Butley Oysterage, an excellent oyster house and smoked fish restaurant, has placed Orford on the map for more modern visitors than the village's more ancient attractions. And deservedly so, for it is an institution that never fails to please – provided you have the foresight to book one of the plain little tables in the dining room. The Oysterage is no longer a secret; it may be packed to the gills even on a winter weekday. But if it is, there is always the opportunity to buy oysters, kippers and smoked salmon from the little retail side of the operation, or the chance for lunch in one of the local pubs.

Orford is a most pleasant spot, the starting point of endless aimless walks in the balmy days of summer or a haven of total isolation during winter weekends when a bitter, bracing wind blows off the North Sea. This is the harsh, unbending east coast of Britain where one can sense the change in

Orford Castle keep

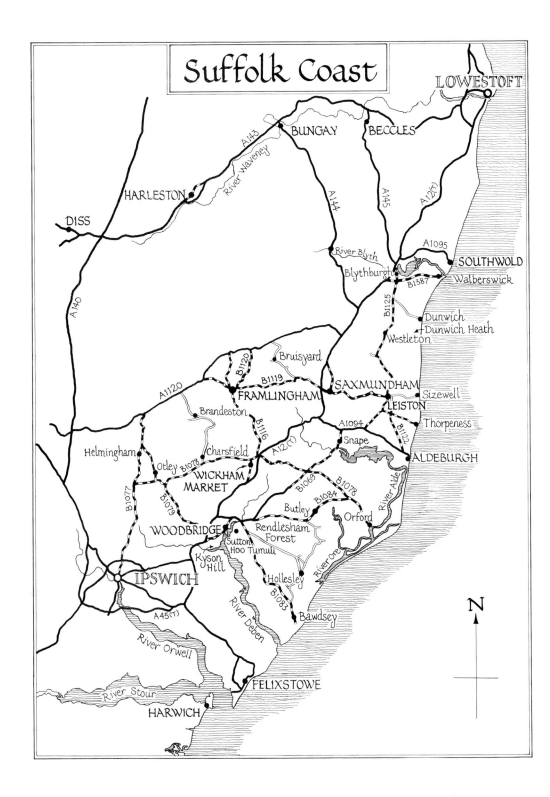

the people as much as in the environment. Here are the eerie coastal villages which appear so often in the ghost stories of M. R. James, the Cambridge don who was well versed in excursions into the remote Suffolk countryside.

This is another former medieval town which has diminished in stature over the centuries, leaving grand homes and a wide village square that speak of a community of different proportions to the one we can see today. The village itself is now some way from the sea, but there is an agreeable walk from the village square to the remaining quay on the river where small pleasure craft bob merrily and the Jolly Sailors pub serves good beer and sandwiches. This is another Mecca for bird-watchers in pursuit of the creatures of the estuary.

In the village stands the surviving keep of Orford Castle, built in the 12th century by Henry II as part of his coastal defence network. The romantic Norman keep is well preserved and of some substance, with ten foot thick walls and three immense turrets. It houses an exhibition on Orford and the local coastline. The parish church, part of which is in ruins, has an interesting interior and was the scene of the premieres of Britten's *Noye's Fludde* and *Curlew River.*

Admirers of castles should journey briefly inland, to Framlingham which has a 12th-century castle fit to act as a backdrop for any fairytale. Framlingham looks virtually as it did in the 12th century, apart from a few odd Tudor chimneys which were added in the 16th century. There are 13 towers linked by a continuous curtain wall, with views of the town and the adjoining lake from the ramparts. The castle was later used as a prison then a school and poor house; an exhibition in the surviving 18th-century poor house tells the history of the castle. A pretty cobbled market square apart, Framlingham has nothing else to offer.

Aldeburgh

Between Orford and Aldeburgh lies Snape, best known for the Maltings on the banks of the River Alde with its famous concert hall and the annual Aldeburgh Festival of Music and Arts held each June. Snape is managed by the Aldeburgh Foundation which is also responsible for the Britten-Pears School for Advanced Musical Studies. Benjamin Britten and Peter Pears were both lovers of the Suffolk coastline and lived nearby. Several Britten compositions reflect the rugged landscape of the area as well as the opera *Peter Grimes,* about a blunt, tortured Suffolk fisherman, the introverted local character. Snape is open throughout the year, with shops, galleries, a pub and cafe, though the concert hall, which is renowned for its fine acoustics, is only open to parties. In addition to the annual festival, there are master classes and concerts at the Maltings throughout the year. It is almost impossible to find a room in the area during the period of the annual festival, making pre-booking essential.

Aldeburgh, on the coast a few miles east, is a genial little holiday resort of parochial charm. The Suffolk poet George Crabbe was born here in 1745 and it was from his poem 'The Borough' that Britten extracted the story of Peter Grimes. There is an ancient town hall, the Moot Hall, which is mainly 16th-century and another handsome Perpendicular church.

Snape Maltings

Smuggling and fishing were the traditional trades of Aldeburgh for centuries. The former may have died out, but little fishing boats are still launched daily from the shingle beach and sell their catches to all-comers as soon as they return.

Leave the town along the B1122 through Leiston. Thorpeness, on the coast, is an unremarkable Edwardian holiday village; nearby Sizewell is the remote location of a nuclear power station.

Dunwich

There is little sign today of the great port which once flourished as Dunwich, a community which, had it survived, would probably have been one of the largest ports on the east coast. All that remains is a handful of houses, an excellent local museum and an abundance of local anecdotes which place Dunwich firmly in the history books long after the port had dwindled in size.

Dunwich began as a Roman settlement, grew into a Saxon town and finally developed as an important medieval port, handling goods from

Europe and beyond. Then, in 1328, the harbour was destroyed in a storm and the merchant ships looked elsewhere. What had been a rich mercantile community was ruined almost overnight. The population dwindled from 4,000 to 100 by the 18th century while cliff erosion claimed virtually all the old town's buildings.

Through a political quirk, however, Dunwich retained its right to send two members of Parliament to Westminster. As a hamlet of 100 citizens, it had political representation equivalent to that of a city like Ipswich, a perfect formula for the creation of the 'rotten borough', a corrupt practice of electing MPs through the purchase of votes. Few places were more rotten than Dunwich. MPs were elected by freemen of the borough; freemen elected each other and did not need to reside in Dunwich to have a vote. The abuse of the Dunwich vote was pioneered in the 17th century by Alderman John Benefice who went under the title – of which he approved – 'King John of Dunwich'. MPs bought their way into Parliament and were abruptly ejected when they fell out of the 'King's' favour. The culprits were outsiders elected as freemen, a fact greatly resented by those living in Dunwich who occasionally resorted to violence in defence of their claims to run their own borough.

The most famous family to be involved in Dunwich borough politics was the Downings, met in Cambridge at the college which, somewhat fortuitously, bears their name. Sir George Downing was a ruthless Dunwich landowner and MP, jailing tenants who did not pay the dubious taxes which he imposed and ejecting freemen from their homes when they would not vote for him. By devious means he was able to sell the second seat in Dunwich to the highest bidder at each election and eventually sold his own seat for £1,200 – a fortune in the 18th century. And so the bribery and corruption continued, until the Reform Act of 1932 which disenfranchised the rotten borough.

The colourful past of Dunwich is well documented in the charming little village museum which has, among other items, several interesting pamphlets on aspects of local history and finds from the seabed during marine archeology expeditions. There is a footpath along the cliffs and steps down to the shore, a good village pub, and the ruins of the old Greyfriars Priory, built in the 13th century and dissolved by Henry VIII. The home of Sir George Downing was on part of the priory estate but it was demolished more than 150 years ago.

Dunwich Heath, south of the village, comprises 214 acres of cliffs and heathland and a mile of beach owned by the National Trust with facilities for birdwatching, walking and fishing. The heath is open all year, with a small charge for cars during summer, and is signposted off the Dunwich to Westleton road about a mile south of Dunwich.

Southwold

From Dunwich, rejoin the main London to Great Yarmouth road, the A12, at Blythburgh where the beautiful, imposing bulk of the great Perpendicular church of the Holy Trinity dominates the bleak marsh landscape. This is another of those stranded giants seen elsewhere in the area, grandiose constructions which seem to bear no relation to their modern surroundings. The tower is 14th-century, the body of the church a century or so younger, but it is the location that is most breathtaking.

Across the marshes and the River Blyth lies Southwold, the largest and most interesting coastal community of the Suffolk coast, a town of distinct character, spotless and a touch pernickety, like a retired colonel put out to grass, with half a mind on golf and the other on a good English lunch. Southwold sits on its clifftop largely unmoved by the outside world, save for the activities of a few welcome hoteliers who have started to replace the traditional tedious fare of the old-fashioned Suffolk hotel with something a little more interesting.

The Victorians loved Southwold and adopted it as one of East Anglia's most pleasing coastal resorts. The era of commercialisation never reached Southwold; even its little railway link with the outside world closed in 1929. Where one might have expected to find a promenade of amusement arcades and candy floss stalls there is the bright white Victorian lighthouse and a wide choice of bracing walks. This is the home of one of East Anglia's most famous breweries, Adnams, and the aroma of their bitter mingles with the tang of the sea daily. Local fish and chips or a crab sandwich, washed down with a pint of Adnams bitter, is as good an English lunch as you will find anywhere in the country. Sadly, individual visits to the brewery are not encouraged.

The church of St Edmund is rated by some as one of the greatest Perpendicular churches in the country. Note the interesting 15th-century clock in which the armoured figure of 'Southwold Jack' strikes the bell with an axe, and the impressive hammerbeam roof. There is a good town museum, the lifeboat museum has an interesting collection of models, relics and old photographs and the sailors' reading room maintains a library of maritime books.

Several houses in Southwold display a distinct Dutch influence in the use of gables – the town museum being one example. The use of Dutch styles became fashionable during the 17th century, though the town overlooks the scene of one of the most bloody battles between English and Dutch forces, the Battle of Sole Bay in 1672 which is commemorated in the town museum. On Gun Hill, near the lighthouse, stand six much-photographed cannon dating from 1740, supposedly a gift of the Duke of Cumberland for the town's defence.

There is one walk in particular which should be made from Southwold. Follow the coastal road south to the River Blyth, through low marshland. At the tip of the river there is, in the summer, a small rowboat ferry for pedestrians only, operating from 9am to 12.30pm and 2pm to 5pm. The village on the southern bank, Walberswick, is another former port now diminished in stature to a pleasant little seaside village in atmospheric countryside with an excellent beach. From here the route continues west to Blythburgh and the main road. Retracing one's steps along this path could occupy an energetic half day with lunch in Blythburgh.

Southwold, Suffolk

Tourist Information

The Cinema
High Street
Aldeburgh
Tel: 072885 3637
Easter-Sept, Mon-Sat 10-1, 2.15-5.15.

Town Hall
Southwold
Tel: 0502 722366
Mid May-mid Sept, Mon-Sat 10-1,
2-4.30.

The Esplanade
Lowestoft
Tel: 0502 565989
Mid Sept-mid May, Mon-Fri 9-1, 2-4.30; mid
May-mid Sept, daily 10-5.30.

Marine Parade
Great Yarmouth
Tel: 0493 846345
Apr 29-May 26, weekdays and Sun, 10-1, 2-5;
May 27-Sept 24, Mon-Sat 9.30-5.30, Sun 12-5;
Sept 24-Oct 8, weekdays and Sun 10-1, 2-5.

Hotels

Seckford Hall
Woodbridge
Tel: 03943 85678
Luxurious Tudor mansion, reputedly once
visited by Elizabeth I, with 34 acres of
grounds. Pleasant river walks to
Woodbridge. Trout fishing in estate lake.
Restaurant speciality lobster, from own
vivarium.
Rooms: 23
Credit cards: Access, Visa, Diners, Amex
Rating ★★★★

The Crown
Thorofare
Woodbridge
Tel: 03943 4242
Modern hotel extension to traditional
coaching house now run by THF.
Rooms: 20
Credit cards: Access, Visa, Diners, Amex
Rating ★★★★

Crown and Castle
Orford
Tel: 0394 450205
Small THF country hotel close to Orford
Castle – booking advisable.
Rooms: 19
Credit cards: Access, Visa, Diners, Amex
Rating★★★★

The Crown
Market Hill
Framlingham
Tel: 0728 723521
Market square coaching inn with character.
THF.
Rooms: 14
Credit cards: Access, Visa, Diners, Amex
Rating ★★★★

The Brudenell
The Parade
Aldeburgh
Plush beachside accommodation. THF.
Rooms: 47
Credit cards: Access, Visa, Diners, Amex
Rating ★★★★

The Crown
High Street
Southwold
Tel: 0502 722275
Small coaching inn owned by Adnams now
restored to offer comfortable
accommodation. See also under restaurants.
Rooms: 12
Credit cards: Access, Visa, Diners, Amex
Rating ★★★

The Swan
Southwold
Newly restored classic hotel also owned by
Adnams and run along the same lines.
Rooms: 45

Credit cards: Access, Visa, Diners, Amex
Rating ★★★

Private Accommodation

Otley House
Otley
nr Ipswich
Tel: 047 339 253
Lovely 17th-century house with piano and
billiards room. Scandinavian flavour to
evening meals.
Rooms: 4
Credit cards: none
Rating ★★★

The Old Rectory
Campsea Ashe
Woodbridge
Tel: 0728 746524
Large village house in four acres; food by
owner, a former professional chef and
restaurateur. See also under restaurants.
Rooms: 7
Credit cards: Access, Visa, Diners, Amex
Rating ★★★

High Poplars
Hinton
Darsham
Saxmundham
Elizabethan farmhouse well situated for the
coast. Narrow staircase unsuitable for the
elderly or arthritic.
Rooms: 4
Credit cards: none
Rating ★★

Restaurants

The Crown
Southwold
Tel: 0502 722275
The showpiece of the Adnams empire.
Excellent bar food with a menu changing
daily – lemon sole with apricots and shallots,
leg of duck with loganberry sauce are
typical dishes. Fixed price menu in the
restaurant includes a different wine with

each course from the extensive and
interesting Adnams cellars. Highly
recommended.
Credit cards: Access, Visa, Diners, Amex
Rating ★★★

The Old Rectory
Campsea Ashe
Woodbridge
Tel: 0728 746524
Winner of the Suffolk Restaurant of the
Year award in 1987, the Old Rectory offers
an imaginative fixed price menu changing
daily. Modern English cooking with French
influences.
Credit cards: Access, Visa, Diners, Amex
Rating ★★★

The Captain's Table
3 Quay Street
Woodbridge
Tel 03943 3145
Long established seafood restaurant,
serving local lobster and other seasonal
dishes. Closed Sundays in winter and all day
Monday.
Credit cards: Access, Visa, Diners, Amex
Rating ★★★

Butley-Orford Oysterage
Market Hill
Orford
Tel: 0394 450277
Famous yet modest fish restaurant, smoking
its own fish and rearing its own oysters.
Simply superb, but be sure to book.
Credit cards: Access, Visa
Rating ★★

Food and Drink

Iletts Farm
Debach House
nr Woodbridge
Tel: 047 337 260
Natural ice cream and dairy products from
own herd. Open daily.

Bruisyard Wines
Church Road
Bruisyard
Saxmundham
Tel: 072875 281
Produces Bruisyard St Peter wine from a
ten-acre vineyard. Wine and herbs for sale,
gardens, play area and free tasting for
visitors. Easter to end Nov, daily 10.30-5.

Shawsgate Vineyard
Badingham Road
Framlingham
Tel: 0728 724060
Guided tour, tasting and vineyard walk.
Picnic area. Apr-Oct, daily 10-5.

The Suffolk Cider Company
The Cider House
Bridge Farm
Friday Street
Brandeston
Woodbridge
Tel: 07882 537
Guided tours of cidermaking house all year,
Mon-Fri at 10, 11, 12, 2, 3 and 4. Shop open
Apr-Sept, Mon-Fri 9.30-5.30, Sat 10-1 and
2-4.

Historic Houses

Otley Hall
Otley
8m NE Ipswich
Tel: 047 339 264.
Picturesque Tudor moated hall with
extensive gardens. National Trust. Mar 26,
27, May 28, 29, Aug 27, 28, 2-6. Groups by
arrangement.

Gardens

Akenfield
1 Park Lane
Charsfield
1m W Wickham Market
Lush council house garden made famous
through television appearances. Homemade wine. May-Sept, daily 10-7.

Ancient Monuments

Framlingham Castle
Framlingham
Imposing castle with 13 towers from the
12th century, once the home of Mary
Tudor. EH. Mar-Sept, daily 10-6; winter,
daily ex. Mon 10-4.

Orford Castle
Orford
Coast fortification from the 12th century
with 90ft polygonal keep. EH. Mar-Sept
daily 10-6; winter daily ex. Mon 10-4.

Sutton Hoo
nr Woodbridge
Tel: 0394 437673
The site of the famous excavation; treasure
is in British Museum with replicas in Ipswich
Museum. Apr-Sept, Sat, Sun and Bank Hol
Mon 2-4. Guided tours 2.15 and 3.15.

Museums

Aldeburgh Moot Hall
Aldeburgh
Small collection of local artefacts in a
timbered 16th-century seafront house. Apr-
Oct, Wed, Sat, Sun, Bank Hols 2.30-5;
winter, Sun 2.30-5.

Dunwich Museum
Dunwich
4m SW Southwold
Devoted to the past of the town which now
lies underneath the waves of the North Sea.
Mar-Oct, Sat and Sun, May-Sept, Tues,
Thurs, Sat and Sun; Aug daily; 2-4.30.

Easton Farm Park
3m W Wickham Market
Rare farm animals including Suffolk Punch
horses, vintage farm machinery, nature trail,
playground. Easter-end Sept, daily 10.30-6.

**Dunwich Underwater Exploration
Exhibition**
The Craft Shop
Front Street
Orford
Record of underwater investigations by
marine archeologists into sunken Dunwich.
All year, daily 11.30-5.

Southwold Museum
Southwold
Local history collections. May-Sept, daily
2.30-4.30.

Museum of Grocery Shop Bygones
70 High Street
Wickham Market
Tel: 0728 747207
Engagingly eccentric collection of bits and
bobs from old grocery stores. Wed-Fri, Sat
10-12.30, 2.30-4.30. Or by appointment.

Woodbridge Museum
Market Hill
Woodbridge
One of the more interesting local museums,
with records of the town's maritime history
and the excavation of Sutton Hoo. Mar-Oct,
Thur-Sat 11-4, Sun 2.30-4.30.

Wildlife Parks and Reserves

Dunwich Heath
Dunwich
National Trust-owned beach and heathland
with information centre and shop. All year.

Havergate Island
Orford
Rare chance to see breeding avocets.
Permits required in advance from Warden,
30 Mundays Lane, Orford IP12 2LX,
enclose sae.

Minsmere
Dunwich
RSPB sanctuary covering 1,500 acres of
beach, marsh and woodland with well-
placed hides. Daily ex. Tues 9-9.

Walks

Waveney District Walks
Routes of varying difficulty around Dunwich
and Beccles. Booklet 45p from Lowestoft.

Other Diversions

Snape Maltings Concert Hall
Snape
5m NW Aldeburgh
Tel: 072 885 2935
Concert hall founded by Benjamin Britten
and Peter Pears. World famous music
school, annual festival each June. Tickets
often sold out within days. Shops and
refreshments, tours for groups only.

Pulls Ferry, Norwich

5 Norwich and the Norfolk Broads

Dominated by the familiar spire of its cathedral, Norwich is a beautiful and historic county city of character, set within a loop of the River Wensum. There are interesting city walks through the old, narrow streets and by the river, and a wealth of medieval buildings. Boat trips regularly leave the city to join the River Yare into the Norfolk Broads, a network of man-made waterways which cover much of east Norfolk to the coast. The 125 miles of navigable waterways of the Broads have a wide range of wildlife, from waterfowl to Britain's largest butterfly, the Swallowtail, and are now protected by their own local authority. Guided water excursions by local naturalists can be booked and it is also possible to hire small day boats. On the coast lies the bustling seaside resort of Great Yarmouth which still retains the interesting old quarter of South Quay and is a busy fishing port, producing some of the best smoked fish in England. Norwich is a good base for the area, and a pleasant place to stroll in the evening. Yarmouth will appeal to those who like traditional seaside resorts. Either provides easy access into the Broads, and there is no practical reason why more than one base is needed for the area.

Norwich

In those periodic and somewhat suspect surveys of the quality of life conducted by arms of the EEC, Norwich invariably comes close to the top of the field as one of the most pleasant cities in Britain. It is not hard to see why. Most of England's county towns have not fared the 20th century well, having allowed modern developments to sweep away the essential character of commercial centres formed, for the most part, by the trading patterns of busy medieval communities. Norwich is one of those rare and welcome exceptions which, by and large, has accepted the new, but not at the expense of the old. It is still easy to discern the form of ancient Norwich in the busy warren of modern streets and to sense a separate identity here. The result is a city which has many sights but is equally pleasurable to the casual walker. Guided walks are organised by the tourist information centre.

The fertile, flat agricultural lands of Norfolk created the wealth of Norwich, riches that gave birth to a thriving mercantile class in the Middle Ages and leave a heritage of fine buildings today, the majority of them in the north east part of the 'Wensum Loop'. Parts of the city walls, which once enclosed a square mile, just as those of the City of London did, still remain.

The castle is a good place to begin a tour of Norwich on foot. Norman in origin, it now serves as the principal regional museum, with displays on archeology, art, ceramics and glass, natural history and social history. The imposing square keep dates from the early 12th century and served as the county's principal jail for more than 600 years until 1887. In front of the castle is the turn of the century Royal Arcade, a distinguished row of shops, which leads to Gentleman's Walk on the east side of the Market Place, busy with stalls from Monday to Saturday. The City Hall here is, according to Pevsner, the finest of English public buildings to be erected between the wars. The bronze doors depict the various industries associated with the city since medieval times. To the south of the Market Place is Theatre Street. The Theatre Royal here is of little architectural interest – it was built in 1935 though a theatre has existed here since the mid 18th century – but of considerable artistic merit, since it is one of the most successful provincial theatres in the country, with a busy repertoire of productions, both serious and light. Next to the theatre is the lovely Georgian Assembly House, built in 1754 as a meeting place for Norwich gentry. Today it serves as a busy arts centre, with gallery, cinema, musical events and a cafe.

To the north of the Market Place, in Charing Cross, is Strangers' Hall, a fascinating former mansion now turned into a museum which depicts domestic life of various periods from the 16th century onwards. The hall has a 13th-century undercroft and a 15th-century great hall, while other additions are as late as Georgian. The odd name comes from its association with Flemish weavers who fled Europe in the 16th and 17th centuries because of religious persecution. They settled throughout East Anglia where they were regarded as strangers, that is non-natives, by the Norwich population. From here St Andrews Street leads east revealing, on the right, Bridewell Alley, still essentially a medieval shopping street. The Bridewell, once a medieval merchant's house, is now another excellent outpost of the Norfolk Museum Service, housing a display which illustrates the trades and industries of the city over the past 200 years. Bridewell Alley houses a unique shop which is also connected with a traditional Norwich trade. The Mustard Shop is dedicated to the condiment that made the Norwich company of Colmans world famous, and stocks several unusual mustards unavailable elsewhere.

Return down St Andrews Hill to St Andrews Street. On the corner stand St Andrews and Blackfriars Halls. These are former churches which are now occupied by restaurants and used for civic exhibitions and craft fairs. St Andrews is a fine example of the Perpendicular style and was once the church of the city's Dominican community; the adjoining Blackfriars Hall was the church's chancel. It is only a few yards from here down St George Street to the river, spanned by an elegant stone Portland bridge designed

Elm Hill, Norwich

by Sir John Soane in 1784. From the bridge are visible the medieval backs of the houses of Elm Hill. Turn right into Colegate then recross the river by the Fye Bridge. Elm Hill is on the right, a cobbled medieval street that has consumed many miles of photographic film over the past century. The picturesque houses now normally have Victorian shop fronts; an exception is the 16th-century Strangers' Club, allegedly once visited by Elizabeth 1. This is a private club which must, by its rules, admit a certain number of members who do not come from Norwich. The pretty former pub here, the Britons Arms, is now an excellent coffee shop at which to break a walking tour of the city.

The best known sight of Norwich has been left till last. The cathedral lies off Tombland, the picturesque street reached by turning left into Princes Street at the top of Elm Hill. Only Salisbury has a higher spire, and, viewed from the two closes by which one approaches, there is an air of grandeur about the building as a whole which says much about the significance of Norwich in the medieval scheme of affairs. Cambridge, it should be noted, has nothing so grand.

The cathedral is essentially Norman and little changed over the centuries. There is an audio-visual display in the visitor's centre, the cloisters are famous for their decorative work and there are some notable carved choir stalls from the 15th century. These things apart, Norwich cathedral, like the city it serves, is charming without being showy. The stone, it should be noted, is not local; it was imported from Caen in Normandy by the Norman builders who began work on the cathedral a mere three years after William was triumphant at Hastings. As happened in Ely, their calculations about the construction of a spire were mistaken and the original structure collapsed in the 14th century. The present spire, 315 feet high, dates from the 15th century and is a familiar icon of the city. The grounds house Norwich School, once attended by a young Horatio Nelson, and pupils form the cathedral choir. In the grounds, at the east end, visitors are still directed to the grave of Edith Cavell, the British nurse who was executed by the Germans during the First World War for helping Allied soldiers to escape from occupied Belgium.

There remains one more pleasant walk which should not be missed. Return to the river by Palace Street and join the riverside path. This leads past Cow Tower, an ancient toll station and the 14th-century Bishops Bridge to Pulls Ferry, once the ancient watergate to the cathedral. The arch once spanned a small canal used to ferry goods into the heart of the city. Further south is the yacht station, a reminder that Norwich lives close to the river and that the Broads are only round the corner.

Norwich Cathedral

The Broads

Nowhere in the United Kingdom has a geographical feature to match the Norfolk Broads, an area of misty fens, abundant wildlife and, it must be said, a touch of Barnum and Bailey showmanship in the areas which attract most interest from tourists. Just a few miles by boat from the heart of Norwich can lead the visitor into a strange, lush landscape of tangled, man-made channels, more than 200 miles of them in all, forming the country's best-known inland waterway system.

It would be foolish to pretend that there is a better way to see the Broads than by riverboat. Some of the more interesting parts can only be reached by water, while roads in the area are often incapable of taking the level of traffic imposed upon them during the summer. Nevertheless, there are ways in which the visitor by car can explore the Broads more satisfactorily than might first appear and sometimes come away with more insight into this fascinating part of Britain than can be had from a hired cruiser visiting the principal holiday villages of the main Broads.

Before travelling east of Norwich it is worth setting down a few basic facts about the Broads area, since the casual visitor turning up unprepared is likely to be thrown somewhat by the myriad faces, wild and brash, sophisticated and simple, which the Broads present. The network of Broads stretches from Norwich north almost to the coast at Hickling Broad and the length of eastern Norfolk south, beyond Great Yarmouth and Lowestoft to Beccles. The channels, made by medieval excavations for peat, are, for the most part, easily navigable. This led to the creation of the Broads' principal modern industry, tourism, in the form of boat hire companies leasing cruisers for general hire. Broads tourism has declined in the face of foreign competition recently, but the tourist boom has permanently scarred the face of the area, leaving several villages overdeveloped and the water systems of the Broads polluted and often dying.

This was a progressive decline in which the delicate ecological balance of the Broads and rivers was upset by the introduction of phosphates from sewage effluent and nitrates from farm fertilisers. Hard as it may be to believe today, the water of the Broads was, around the turn of the century, almost crystal clear. The introduction of phosphates and nitrates encouraged luxuriant growth and fish life but also turned the waters cloudy as algae took advantage of the new foods available to them. When the algae died, it formed a thick, muddy layer on the bed which eventually killed much of the wildlife. Several Broads are now effectively dead and every remaining waterway has been affected to some degree or another.

The Broads contain some of the richest wildlife in Britain, from rare birds to lovely butterflies and the occasional otter colony. Yet this gradual destruction of the area went largely unnoticed by the public authorities for many years. When the national parks of England and Wales were being set up in the 1940s, the Broads were left out, an action which prompted a public letter of astonishment from one of the most eminent naturalists of this century, Julian Huxley. The decline worsened, aggravated by increasing and unchecked tourism. Only in 1978 did a fledgling Broads Authority come into being, and that lacked satisfactory funding and statutory powers to manage both land and water in the area. In March 1988 the Broads Bill received Royal Assent and set up a new Broads Authority which effectively turned the area into a National Park and a year later the body officially came into being.

Given the scale of environmental problems which the Authority now faces it is little short of scandalous that action was not taken earlier. In addition to the plight of the dead Broads, erosion caused by the wash of pleasure boats is destroying banks by as much as three metres every ten years in some areas. The end of the traditional cutting of the fens for thatching and hay has led to many fen areas, once renowned for their variety of flora and fauna, being invaded by wet woodland, destroying much of the local wildlife. Almost one quarter of the grazing marshland of the Broads has been lost through pressure from the Common Market on farmers to convert grazing land to crops by draining the ground. Wildlife suffered (and the grain was, of course, part of an EEC surplus) and the unique marsh skyline was suddenly interrupted by vast grain barns and electricity pylons.

Happily one can already see that some of this sad tide has now been turned through imaginative conservation

The Broads

areas. The new Authority realises that tourists are necessary for the area and is attempting to assimilate them into the Broads with as little environmental damage as possible. New boats are being designed which produce less wash, research is being funded into ways of encouraging the tiny creatures, such as water fleas, which will devour the algae killing the water, and farmers are being urged to return to traditional methods. Tourists are invited to become familiar with the ecosystem of the Broads through an annual programme of walks, visits and other events. There are already welcome signs that much of the damage done to the area can be reversed and, just as welcome, that the health of the Broads will not be taken for granted by local authorities or the general public in the future.

For the visitor who is not exploring by boat, the northern part of Broadland is by far the most interesting. There will be those who will urge the case for a visit to the southern Broads at any costs, and there is no doubt that they will appeal to the experienced birdwatcher. However, the south is marked by the worst overdevelopment and the least interesting scenery, and, Earsham's excellent Otter Trust apart, would be little missed by the average visitor.

The first stop for any new visitor to Broadland should be the excellent information centre at Ranworth run by the Broads Authority in conjunction with the boat hire firm Blakes. This is one of the few places in the area where the motorist can get a good view of a Broad, and also the place to track down any seasonal events which may be happening. A short walk from the information centre is the Broadland Conservation Centre, reached through a marked nature trail which passes through the different stages of wetland found in the vicinity of the Broads. The centre has a permanent display on the ecology of the area and local wildlife. From the tower of Ranworth church there are magnificent views of the countryside.

There are several interesting places to visit by boat from here. Cockleshoot Broad is a dead Broad which has been made a nature reserve and used as an experimental station to test various ways of reviving dead waterways. The Broad itself is not navigable but can be seen from the Bure. Alternatively it can be reached on foot by a wooden walkway from the riverside car park on the road from Woodbastwick. There is a nature trail and bird hide for visitors. Both Horning and Wroxham are busy boating stations on the Bure, but are not without their charm.

To see more of the area by car, drive east from Ranworth to the little market town of Acle then follow the main road to Caister for two miles before turning left onto the B1152 for Potter Heigham. This is another popular boating centre and one where electric day boats can be hired by

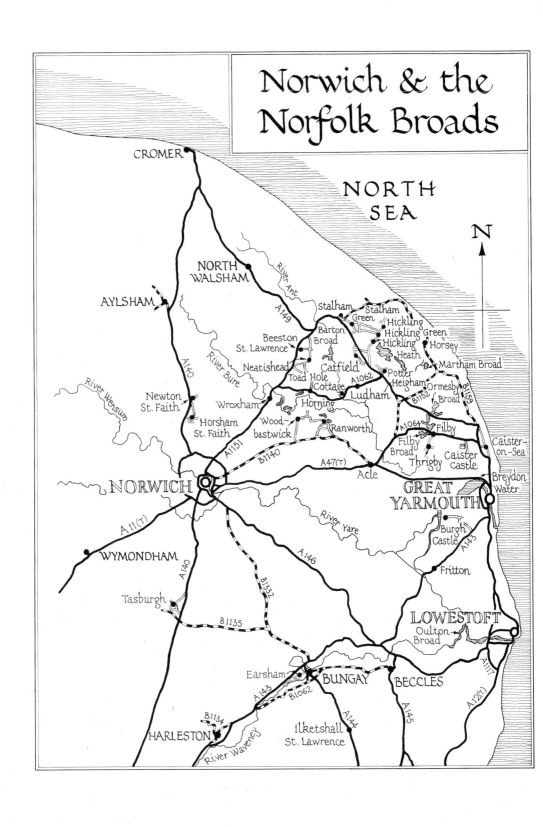

the hour by day visitors. Using one of these day boats it is possible to reach the nature reserves of Hickling, Horsey and the waters of Martham Broad in around 35 minutes. One of the sights of this area is only easily accessible by water – the ruins of St Benet's Abbey south of Ludham. Close to Ludham, on the River Ant, is Toad Hole Cottage, an eel-catcher's cottage which has been turned into a museum of Victorian marsh life by the Broads Authority. There is a wildlife trail and a highly popular water trail which should be booked in advance since seats are limited to eight per journey. The trail consists of a guided journey on a narrow electric boat into the depths of the Ant. At different times of the year, marsh harriers, cormorants, swallowtail butterflies and an enormous variety of wild flowers can be seen, and the experienced guide will point out the various sights during the journey.

If time is short, the main A1062 will take you back to Horning and Wroxham for the main road to Norwich. Alternatively, for a longer but more picturesque exit, travel north, through Catfield, across the main A149 road, to Hickling Green for a view of Hickling Broad, the largest lake in Broadland, popular with wildfowl and yachtsmen alike. The minor road to Stalham Green then rejoins the A149 at Stalham. Turn the corner over the Ant and then join the minor road to Neatishead which leads to Horning and the main roads out of the area.

This is just a compressed introduction to the complexities of the Broads, but it is designed to whet the appetite of anyone who might feel minded to return later.

Great Yarmouth

The biggest and brashest resort of East Anglia lies at the eastern perimeter of the Broads. Of Great Yarmouth Dickens had Peggotty in *David Copperfield* remark that it was 'upon the whole, the finest place in the universe'. One wonders whether the author would share the same sentiments today, but Yarmouth, for all its gaudiness, is more interesting than might appear at first glance and is well placed as a base for exploring the Broads and Norwich.

Yarmouth has been 'Great' since the 13th century when it was a busy mercantile harbour and herring port. The old town was built on a sandbank washed up between the River Yare and the sea, a geographical arrangement which can still be seen in a plan of the modern town. This can be rather confusing for the modern visitor who is drawn, inevitably, to the seafront, only to find the long Marine Parade of amusement arcades, theatres and tourist kiosks facing a vast, golden beach... and little else. Old Yarmouth is somewhere else completely, on the west side of the spit of land adjoining the Yare. It was here that the medieval port thrived in a lively and gregarious seaman's community that was known to mariners throughout Europe.

Modern Yarmouth remains a busy port, both for cargo and fish. Herrings are still important and you will find some of the finest kippers to be smoked in England on the stalls of the Yarmouth fishmonger (and the breakfast menu of any worthwhile hotel or bed and breakfast establishment). In recent years, oil exploration companies drilling in the North Sea have brought new business to the town and it is by no means unusual to see a platform waving gently offshore only a short distance from the piers of the main holidaymaker's beach. But it is tourism that has transformed Yarmouth most of all, mass domestic tourism of the Kiss Me Quick school. Between the wars and in the 1950s and 1960s Yarmouth prospered as never before, attracting famous television stars to the end-of-the-pier shows and hundreds of thousands of visitors annually into the bed and breakfast rooms of welcoming seaside landladies.

The bubble burst late in the 1960s with the increasing popularity of the cheap package holiday in the Mediterranean, as it did for many traditional English seaside resorts. The seafront of Yarmouth has never quite recovered and, at times, has simply attempted to slap on more greasepaint to cover the aging cracks instead of starting afresh. Nevertheless, there are some unusual discoveries to be made in some of our fading resorts of old, Yarmouth among them. One curiosity is that the slump in tourist business has, as so often happened, brought about a colonisation of the place by a new, immigrant community confident that they can make businesses pay which were unviable for their previous English owners. In the case of Yarmouth, the newcomers are Greek, or to be more precise Greek Cypriots, who are now happily engaged in any number of restaurants, fish and chip bars, newsagents and shops, with a lively and active Cypriot community busily at work in the town. Yarmouth, as the author can testify, is the sort of place where you can eat an excellent kebab on the seafront, drinking retsina and listening to bouzouki music, while the outline of a well-lit, towering oilrig slips slowly past the window, illuminated like a floating Eiffel Tower.

The seafront is the place to stay in Yarmouth; the old town, around the quayside, the area to wander. The one exception is, perhaps, the seafront Maritime Museum of East Anglia, which offers an admirable record of seagoing life over the centuries and will be enjoyed even by those with little interest in the lives of sailors past and present. An exploration of old Yarmouth should begin in the large Market Place, now somewhat diminished by a tedious modern shopping precinct erected next to it. The church of St Nicholas here is most remarkable for the fact that it was almost completely rebuilt in the postwar years following its destruction during a German bombing raid in 1942. The church is said to have the largest floor area of any parish church in England. In the adjoining Church Plain is the small house where Anna Sewell, famous for *Black Beauty*, was born, as well as a handsome Georgian vicarage, and the early 18th-century almshouses of the Fishermen's Hospital.

From the Market Place it is a short walk to the old waterfront of the quay. Once these were unusual for 'the Rows' some 145 tiny alleys, some no more than four feet wide, with houses, grand and modest, on either side. This distinctly cramped building scheme, brought about by the shortage of land in the centre of town, led to the development of a special kind of narrow wheelbarrow which was used to run goods up and down the Rows, a curiosity which can be sometimes seen in old prints of the quay. Most of the Rows were destroyed during heavy wartime bombing, but a few remain around the South Quay amid the most interesting old buildings of Yarmouth.

The Elizabethan House dates from 1596 and contains panelled contemporary rooms and a display of Victorian domestic life. The Old Merchant's House, in one of the remaining Rows, is an English Heritage property from the 17th century, with rooms restored to their original condition and early domestic ironwork. Away from the quay, the Tolhouse Museum has a local history exhibition in the medieval building which was once the town courthouse. The dungeons are preserved and there is a brass rubbing centre. A final curiosity in Yarmouth can be found back from the South Beach Parade: the Nelson monument. Yarmouth erected a column to the memory of Norfolk's great hero in 1819, more than 20 years before the famous column of Trafalgar Square, which is one foot taller, was built. The statue of Britannia at the top faces inland towards Burnham Thorpe, Nelson's birthplace. The admiral was no stranger to Yarmouth; he landed here after the battles of Copenhagen and the Nile.

Tourist Information

The Guildhall
Gaol Hill
Norwich
Tel: 0603 666071
Jan-May, Oct-Dec, Mon-Fri 9.30-5.30, Sat
9.30-1; Jun-Sept, Mon-Sat 9.30-6, Sun 9.30-1.
Guided tours.

1 South Quay
Great Yarmouth
Tel: 0493 846345
Ex Bank Hols, Mon-Thur 9-5.30, Fri 9-5.

Hotels

Georgian House Hotel
32-34 Unthank Road
Norwich
Tel: 0603 615655/617082
Largely Georgian hotel with restaurant close
to the city centre.
Rooms: 18
Credit cards: Access, Visa, Diners, Amex
Rating ★★★

Sprowston Manor Hotel
Wroxham Road
Norwich
Tel: 0603 410871
Country house hotel with restaurant on
eight-acre estate.
Rooms: 41
Credit cards: Access, Visa, Diners, Amex
Rating ★★★★

Hotel Nelson
Prince of Wales Road
Norwich
Tel: 0603 760260
Modern business hotel close to the station.
Rooms: 121
Credit cards: Access, Visa, Diners, Amex
Rating ★★★★

Maid's Head
Tombland

Norwich
Tel: 0603 761111
Traditional upmarket hotel in the centre of
the city.
Rooms: 80
Credit cards: Access, Visa, Diners, Amex
Rating ★★★★

Park Farm Hotel
Hethersett
Norwich
Tel: 0603 810264
Family-run country hotel on the A11 five
miles south of Norwich. French and English
cooking, game and seafood. Indoor pool,
sauna and jacuzzi.
Rooms: 22
Credit cards: Access, Visa, Diners, Amex
Rating ★★★★

Private Accommodation

Mayfield Farm
Long Stratton
10m S Norwich
Tel: 0508 31763
Attractive private 16th-century farmhouse.
Rooms: 2
Credit cards: none
Rating ★★

Restaurants

Brasted's
8-10 St Andrews Hill
Norwich NR2 1AD
Elegant dining room in old Norwich which
combines British and French cooking in a
range of fish and meat dishes, all based on
local produce.
Closed Sundays
Credit cards: Access, Visa, Amex
Rating ★★★★

Tiffins
9 Stonecutters Way
Great Yarmouth
Tel: 0493 852484
A cut above the usual Yarmouth fare. Mainly

French dishes, but with some plainer English originals including Norfolk duck.
Closed Mondays
Credit cards: Access, Visa, Amex
Rating ★★★★

Seafood Restaurant
85 North Quay
Great Yarmouth
Tel: 0493 856009
Long-established seafood house with live lobsters from the tank. The generous shellfish platter is always popular; watch for Greek-style dishes from the Cypriot owners.
Closed Sundays
Credit cards: Access, Visa, Amex
Rating ★★★

Food and Drink

The Mustard Shop
3 Bridewell Alley
Norwich
Tel: 0603 627889
Mustard museum selling several specialist varieties not commonly available, and prints of famous Colman posters. Open shop hours.

The Cider Place
Cherry Tree Farm
Ilketshall St Lawrence
Nr Beccles
Tel: Ilketshall 353
Apple juice and traditional ciders matured in oak barrels. Small selection of country wines. Open daily all year.

L. E. Greenacre & Sons
39 Market Row
Great Yarmouth
Tel: 0493 843138
Superb prize-winning pie maker and butcher. Game pie from local birds made to order. Open daily Mon-Sat.

Historic Houses

Beeston Hall
Beeston
5m NE Norwich
Georgian house with orangery, wine cellars, art gallery and woodland. End Mar-Sept, Fri, Sun, Bank Hols and Wed in August, 2-5.30.

Horsham St Faith
2m N Norwich
Rare 13th-century monastic wall paintings in Benedictine priory founded in 1105. Norman and medieval stonework. Mar-Sept, Sun 2-6; Bank Hols 11-6.

Gardens

Fairhaven Garden Trust
South Walsham
9m NE Norwich
Rare shrubs and water plants by the side of South Walsham Broad. End Mar-May, Sun and Bank Hol; May-Sept, Wed, Sun and Bank Hols, 2-6.

Fritton Lake and Country Park
Great Yarmouth-Beccles road
Outdoor leisure centre in 170 acres with gardens, woodland walks, play areas, pony rides, fishing in season, windsurfing school and wildfowl reserve. End Mar-Oct, 10-6.

Rainthorpe Hall Gardens
Tasburgh
8m S Norwich
Collection of bamboos and other interesting trees in garden of Elizabethan mansion. Plants for sale. May-Sept, Sun and Bank Hols 2-5.30.

Ancient Monuments

Burgh Castle
Great Yarmouth
Minor remains of Roman fort. EH. Easter to Oct, dawn to dusk.

Caister Roman Town
Great Yarmouth
The old Roman commercial port, now a
small collection of ruins. EH. Daily, dawn to
dusk.

Nelson's Monument
Great Yarmouth
Some 217 steps take you to the top of the
144ft tower erected to the famous East
Anglian in 1819. Jul and Aug daily ex. Sat,
2-6.

Museums

Old Merchant's House
Row 111 South Quay
Great Yarmouth
Original merchant's house from the 17th
century. EH. Mar-Sept, daily 10-6. Apply to
custodian in Row 111.

Elizabethan House Museum
South Quay
Great Yarmouth
Fine 16th-century merchant's house with
displays of Victorian domestic life. Jun-Sept,
daily ex. Sat, Oct-May, Mon-Fri, 10-1, 2-5.30.

Tollhouse Museum
Tollhouse Street
Great Yarmouth
Dungeons and brass rubbing in what was
once the town jail. Oct-May, Mon-Fri, Jun-
Sept, daily ex. Sat, 10-1, 2-5.30.

Maritime Museum for East Anglia
Great Yarmouth
Extensive and interesting record of fishing,
trading and shipbuilding in the region. Oct-
May, Mon-Fri 10-1, 2-5.30; Jun-Sept, daily ex.
Sat 10-5.30.

Castle Museum
Norwich
Regional museum, local and international
items from Egyptology to ceramics and fine
art. Mon-Sat 10-5, Sun 2-5.

Strangers' Hall Museum of Domestic Life
Norwich
Recreations of 16th- to 19th-century
domestic life in a medieval townhouse.
Mon-Sat 10-5.

The Bridewell Museum
Bridewell Alley
Norwich
The traditional trades and professions of
Norwich recollected. Mon-Sat 10-5.

John Jarrold Printing Museum
Whitefriars
Norwich
Tel: 0603 660211
Techniques of printing through the ages in
a 12th-century crypt. Jul-Sept, Tues 10-4.
Other times by appointment.

St Peter Hungate Church Museum and
Brass Rubbing Centre
Princes Street
Norwich
Brass rubbing, church art and furnishings
in one of the city's 36 medieval churches.
Mon-Sat 10-5.

Wildlife Parks and Reserves

The Butterfly Farm
Marine Parade
Great Yarmouth
Tropical gardens, birds and butterflies
under glass. Mar-Nov, daily 10-dusk.

Norfolk Wildlife Park & Play Centre
Witchingham
12m NW Norwich
Claimed to be the largest collection of
British and European wildlife in the
country. Natural enclosures cover 40 acres.
All year, daily 10-6 or dusk.

Otter Trust
Earsham
nr Bungay
Breeding collection of European otters for

reintroduction to the wild. Muntjack and Chinese water deer, wildfowl. Apr-Oct daily 10.30-6.

Thrigby Hall Wildlife Gardens
nr Filby
5m NW Great Yarmouth
Snow leopards, Asian deer and birds in landscaped gardens. All year, daily 10-5 or dusk.

Flatford Mill, Stour Valley

6 The Stour Valley, Colchester and Ipswich

'Constable Country' is the area of outstanding natural beauty around the valley of the River Stour, the subject of many of Constable's great paintings of the English countryside. Several places painted by Constable can still be seen, most notably Flatford Mill and Willy Lott's Cottage. Constable's fellow Suffolk artist Thomas Gainsborough was born in nearby Sudbury and often painted the Stour valley, though he is best known for his portraits. This area is easily joined with the journey to mid Suffolk (see p. 57), and there are several links between the two in the stories of Gainsborough and Constable and their work. Two of Britain's best known luxury country hotels, Hintlesham Hall and Maison Talbooth, are situated in the area. Although both Colchester and Ipswich are busy modern towns, they possess interesting older quarters. There is little need to book more than one hotel as a base for exploring Constable Country, and for many that base will be Dedham itself. None of the local sights is more than an hour's drive away.

The Stour Valley

The verdant landscape of the Stour Valley, dividing Essex from Suffolk, comes as something of a shock for those approaching from the south.

After miles of the tedious and uninviting flatland which typifies so much of north east Essex, the views are abruptly altered. An idyllic English countryside appears, albeit one which the pressure of modern traffic has punctured with the busy A12. This part of East Anglia has survived most of the pressures of modern development remarkably well. Constable's paintings have their part to play in this, for without their ever popular visual record of an earlier, quieter Suffolk, the temptation to thrust out the boundaries of Colchester and Ipswich even further might have been irresistible. Constable placed this part of East Anglia in the national – and international – consciousness as an image of rural England at a time when Suffolk was a little-known backwater, and the Stour valley has stayed there ever since. Whether the modern housing estates would have been deterred had Constable looked elsewhere for his inspiration is a matter for some speculation. One need not travel far from the quiet streets of Dedham and other villages in the area to find post-war development of the worst kind.

The obvious starting place for a visit to this area is one of the famous luxury hotels. This will not suit everyone's pockets, but there are some inexpensive private houses and cheaper hotels in the bustling cities of Ipswich and Colchester. The distances around here are not great, making the Dedham area in particular a popular weekend break for Londoners. Reservations for hotels and the few worthwhile rural restaurants are advisable at weekends throughout the year.

The heart of Constable country is Dedham Vale, a lovely stretch of the Stour passing Stratford St Mary, Dedham and Flatford, and close to Constable's birthplace in East Bergholt. The artist said of the area 'I love every stile and stump and lane... these scenes made me a painter and I am grateful... I had often thought of pictures of them before I ever touched a pencil.'

The best way to approach the Vale is on foot. A network of little paths link all the main points of interest which can be seen, at a comfortable walking pace, in a single, happy day, with lunch in one of the several local pubs. Dedham is an obvious starting place, a quiet, prosperous little town with a lovely High Street and a famous church. One can still – just – imagine the scene when the artist himself, boarding the coach for London here, heard the Vale described by a fellow traveller as 'Constable's Country'. Modern Dedham remains an artist's town; there is an active painting school with regular exhibitions of local artists who follow in the giant footsteps of Constable.

The town owes its present grandeur to the wool trade. It was an

103

Dedham, Suffolk

important weaving and dyeing centre for centuries, and a busy stopping place on the old main road from London to the East Anglian coast. In the 17th century the wool trade declined, leaving Dedham with an abundance of lovely buildings and a church more in keeping with a large town than a rural backwater. The parish church of St Mary dominates the handsome High Street and is a sure indication of the wealth which medieval Dedham possessed. The stone for facing the walls was imported in the late 15th century from Caen in Normandy and the whole church finished in the space of 30 years from the donations of important local wool trade families. The High Street boasts several fine buildings. The Georgian house called Sherman's was once a school founded by the wool trader Edmund Sherman. His family were early emigrants to America; a famous descendant was General William T. Sherman who fought in the Civil War. The Marlborough Head is a 16th-century half-timbered inn, while the nearby Sun is an archetypal coaching inn. The Dedham Centre, in a former Congregational church in the High Street, has a small toy museum and several local craft shops.

From the war memorial a path known as the Drift leads past the tourist information centre to the recreation ground and past the half-timbered Flemish Houses to Castle Hill. On the corner with East Lane stands Castle House, the home of another local painter, Sir Alfred Munnings, President of the Royal Academy from 1944 to 1949, known in his day for horse and sporting pictures. An exhibition of his work is open to view in the house periodically during the summer. Return down the hill into Crown Street, then Brook Street. On the right, marked, is the footpath for Flatford Mill, a mile and a half away. Constable's father owned the mill and the property opposite, Valley Farm, and the young artist briefly worked on the mill. This was the scene of *The Haywain* and *Willy Lott's Cottage*. The latter remains, under the control of the National Trust, but is closed to the public. Bridge Cottage, seen in one of the artist's pencil sketches, now has a display about Constable's life and work. The bridge itself is a reconstruction, copied from the artist's depiction of its predecessor.

Enthusiastic walkers can continue east at Flatford, finally arriving at the town of Manningtree after some three miles. There is little to see but one abiding anecdotal link. The town was the birthplace of Matthew Hopkins, a zealous lawyer who was appointed Witchfinder General for East Anglia and, in this capacity, condemned more than 400 women to death. Hopkins was eventually caught by his own tricks; tried as a sorcerer then hanged in 1647.

To the north lies the little village of half-timbered houses where

Stour Valley, Colchester & Ipswich

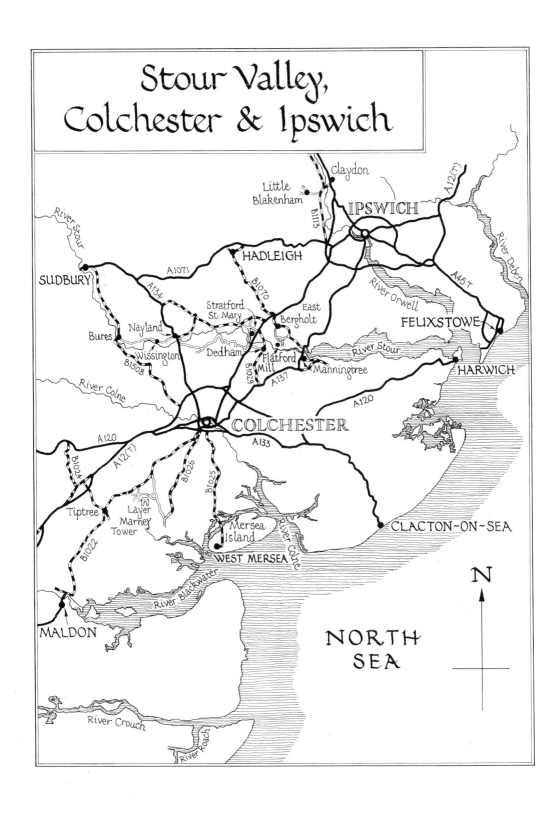

Constable was born, East Bergholt and a pleasant footpath along the northern bank of the Stour, past Dedham Mill, to Stratford St Mary. From here one can return to Dedham by the Talbooth, seen in the painting *Dedham Vale*, and on a footpath to the south of the Stour.

There is a lovely drive from Dedham to Sudbury along the Stour valley. Nayland is a pretty, half-timbered village situated beside the river. There is a rare Constable religious painting, of Christ blessing the bread and wine, in the village church and several imposing houses, the best being Alston Court on Church Street. Neighbouring Wissington has a fetching Norman church with traces of wall paintings. Bures, divided by the Stour, has a 13th- to 15th-century church with several magnificent tombs of local nobles. Queen Elizabeth 1 visited the area twice to see the influential Waldegrave family, a political line to this day, who lived at Smallbridge Hall, now a school. Here the road turns north, to mid-Suffolk and Sudbury.

Nayland, Essex

Colchester

The city of Colchester claims, with some substance, to be the oldest continuously inhabited community in Britain. It was a flourishing Roman garrison long before London was developed and has witnessed two bloody episodes which seem more in keeping with the frontier towns of the Wild West than the coast of Essex.

Modern Colchester is no swan. There has been large scale redevelopment of the city and a surfeit of tasteless commercial construction in and around the ancient heart. But do not be deterred; beyond the multi-storey car parks and shopping malls much of interest remains. The city is certainly worth an afternoon and will also appeal to those whose budgets do not stretch to the Hintlesham Halls of this world and would prefer a greater range of inexpensive restaurants.

There was a celtic settlement known as Camulodunum at this point on the Colne river in the first century BC. One of its rulers, the warrior king Cunobelin, was the model for Shakespeare's Cymbeline. Camulodunum fell to the Romans in AD 44, a year after the invasion, and established the town as a colony for retired soldiers. As related earlier, they were later massacred by Boadicea's rebellious army but the colony was soon restored. The remains of the original wall can still be seen, almost enclosing the old centre of the city, and Colchester retains one of the largest surviving remnants of Roman Brtiain, one of the original gates into the walled city. This is the Balkerne Gate, found off Balkerne Hill, and a good spot to start any walking tour of old Colchester. The gate used to be the western entrance to the city, doubtless well guarded for most of its history. Part of the gate has been absorbed by a neighbouring pub – quite rightly known as the Hole in the Wall – but there is still pedestrian access through an arch. The gate was excavated in 1917; it was probably sealed at the end of the Roman era.

Behind the gate is one of Colchester's most dominant landmarks, the vast Victorian water tower known to everyone as Jumbo, and the way to North Hill which joins the busy High Street. The latter bisects the centre of old Colchester and most interesting sights lie off it. Walking from the gates to the left is what remains of the old Dutch Quarter of the city, now composed of some 50 restored houses dating from the 15th century. West Stockwell Street leads into the quarter, turn through the churchyard of St Martins into East Stockwell Street. Then follow St Helens Lane into Maidenburgh Street which adjoins the castle park. Here a Roman theatre has been uncovered and the outlines can be traced from the remains. In the park itself is the magnificent Norman castle, the keep is in pristine condition, reached by a wooden bridge; its present-day state of repair giving no inkling of the bloody past.

The castle stands on the site of the Roman temple to the emperor/god Claudius which stood at the heart of ancient Camulodunum. It was the taxes levied to pay for this extravagant structure that prompted, in part, the rebellion of Boadicea. During the Dark Ages, the town seems to have prospered on passing trade from the coast to London, and the townspeople were well guarded behind the walls which the Romans had erected. The Normans selected the city as an important garrison point shortly after the invasion of 1066, and Colchester has remained a garrison town to this day. The castle was of classical Norman design, but only the magnificent keep remains. The castle saw little early service as a fortress and was soon converted to prison use. Sir Thomas Malory wrote his chivalrous poem *Morte d'Arthur* while imprisoned here. In the early 17th century, the property was sold and almost destroyed by an eccentric owner who tore down large parts of the structure in a vain search for buried treasure. The keep and ramparts, the latter now turned over to grass, were later saved from further destruction and given to the town. The castle museum contains one of the most important Roman collections in the country.

The centuries of relative peace behind the city walls were shattered by the bloody 11-week siege of 1648 which destroyed many buildings and churches and large sections of the old Roman defences. This was one of the most bitter engagements of the Civil War and one which marked the town for years to come. Colchester had initially declared for Parliament. There was a strong Puritanical streak in the town – as there was in much of East Anglia. Many East Anglian names were registered on the passenger list of the *Mayflower* as it set sail for the New World. But a Royalist force commanded by Lord Goring forced itself on the town on the pretence that it would be gone within days. In reality, the Royalists, and the hapless townsfolk, were soon attacked by the Parliamentary forces under Thomas, Lord Fairfax, and the blockade had begun. Horses, cats and dogs were killed for food as the local population pleaded with the Royalists to surrender.

When the inevitable climbdown came, three of the Royalist officers were executed and 3,531 soldiers and officers below captain's rank were stripped of their possessions. Several hundred townspeople were killed during the conflict; Fairfax fined the largely innocent town £14,000; many people had lost their homes during the bombardment. Several buildings still bear the marks of the siege today. The ruins of the Priory Church of St Botolph, just outside the city walls behind Priory Street, are a visible reminder of the siege. The church was once the parish church of the town, until it became a target for the Parliamentary forces during the siege and reduced to the ruins seen today. The Old Siege House, in East Street, is a fine half-timbered inn on which can be clearly seen the bullet marks of the battle.

The remainder of historic Colchester can be found in the old streets bounded by the High Street to the north, Queen Street, Head Street and St John's Street. Tymperley's is an interesting old house which is now the home of a valuable collection of locally-made clocks. The Elizabethan scientist and doctor, William Gilberd, as famous in his day as Einstein was to the middle decades of the 20th century, once lived in the house. He was a pioneer of research into electromagnetism, a president of the College of Physicians and doctor to Elizabeth I and James I. Nearby Scheregate is a former medieval gate now covered by largely 17th-century buildings. Three other museums in the vicinity deserve mention. Hollytrees, close to the castle, contains domestic objects of the 18th and 19th centuries. All Saints Church, opposite the castle in the High Street, has been converted into an entertaining natural history museum covering the whole of Essex. Another redundant church, 14th-century Holy Trinity in Trinity Square, is now a social history museum with displays of country life and crafts.

It would be wrong to leave Colchester without recording that the city is the birthplace of two of Britain's most enduring nursery rhymes. One stems from the siege, during which an ingenious defender, One Eyed Jack, held back the Parliamentary forces single-handed from the tower of St John's Abbey. The efforts which Fairfax's forces made to dislodge the man – they eventually killed him and destroyed the abbey – were the basis for the rhyme of Humpty Dumpty. And 'Old King Cole' is reputed to have been a local monarch of the second century AD whose daughter, Helena, married a Roman general. Now St Helena – she is said to have discovered the True Cross – is the figure atop the tower of the Town Hall, and the reason why the borough arms show a cross miraculously sprouting into life.

Lovers of seafood will already associate Colchester with oysters. These

Colchester Castle.

are, in fact, farmed on Mersea Island to the south, where they may be bought fresh from tanks by the road. The island is joined to the mainland by a causeway which is impassable at high tide. Layer Marney Tower, six miles south west on the Maldon road, boasts the highest Tudor gatehouse in England and is open periodically during the summer – you will need to check with the tourist office to be certain of hours. Lovers of brash seaside resorts should repair to Clacton which has all of Great Yarmouth's rude qualities without an iota of historic, cultural or natural charm.

Ipswich

It is hard to get excited about modern Ipswich – save for one pre-eminent attraction: Christchurch Park. The county town of Suffolk is almost as old as Colchester. It was a busy Anglo Saxon port with quays on the River Orwell and developed into one of the wealthiest towns in medieval England. Contemporary prints show a beautiful, thriving city of substantial Tudor buildings, earlier churches and religious institutions. Few survived the centuries and, of those that did, many were destroyed during a disastrous redevelopment phase of the 1960s when Ipswich was first designated a new town to absorb overspill from London, then abruptly removed from the scheme. The city of today displays some of the worst excesses of modern redevelopment: ugly car parks, grey office developments, and shopping precincts which are dismal in design and utterly lacking in any regional character.

I would advise the visitor to avoid the place altogether were it not for Christchurch Park, one of the most pleasant open spaces in the country and, moreover, one blessed with a fine mansion once visited by Elizabeth 1. Christchurch Mansion was begun in 1548 and now contains an impressive collection of works by both Constable and Gainsborough, as well as displays of period decor, household utensils and costumes. Constable's *Willy Lott's Cottage* will interest anyone who has seen the original location at Flatford Mill. The survival of Christchurch is a story of private generosity, not municipal foresight. The estate was built for the Withipoll family and later owned by the Devereuxs and the Fonnereaus. In 1894 it was sold to a development syndicate and would doubtless have disappeared under a late Victorian housing estate without the intervention of Felix Cobbold, a local banker and member of the brewing family. He bought the house and gave it to Ipswich Corporation on condition that the surrounding park was also purchased, ensuring that future Ipswich retained at least some of its past charm. Sadly, the family of Cobbold has been less well treated by time; the old brewery of Tolly Cobbold was closed by its new multinational owners in 1989 and so another ancient Suffolk name has disappeared.

Having decided to brave the car parks of Ipswich to visit Christchurch Park, it would be unwise to avoid the few remaining sights of the city. St Margaret's Church, in St Margaret's Plain close to the park, is an imposing 15th-century flint and stone edifice with, inside, an astonishing painted hammerbeam roof displaying, among other emblems, the coat of arms of Charles II. Few English churches have an interior of such over ornateness; it is worth opening the door to witness. The most photogenic attraction is the Ancient House in Buttermarket, built in the 15th century but with pargeting dating from the 17th. This is reputed to be the best example of pargeting in the country, and once again the arms of Charles II feature in the plaster carving work. The Great White Horse in Tavern Street is a 16th-century coaching inn, largely rebuilt early in the 19th century, famous for the residency of Dickens who used it for an episode in the *Pickwick Papers*. It has lost much of its individuality over the years.

The East Anglian streak of rebellion has left the city with one of the earliest non-conformist chapels in the country, the Unitarian Meeting House in Friars Street built in 1699. The sparse, clean lines of the timber interior are most impressive and similar to those of churches set up by emigrating East Anglians in New England. Nearby, in St Nicholas Street and Silent Street, can be found Tudor timber-framed houses, while behind the 15th-century church of St Mary at the Elms stand the town's oldest inhabited cottages, dating from 1467. The Ipswich Museum is an energetic institution, displaying replicas of finds from Sutton Hoo and Mildenhall as well as material from the third world and Roman excavations.

Tourist Information

Town Hall
Princes Street
Ipswich
Tel: 0473 258070
All year, Mon-Thur 9-5, Fri 10-4.30; also Apr-Aug Sat 10-4. Guided tours.

1 Queen Street
Colchester
Tel: 0206 46379
May-Sept, Mon-Fri 9-5, Sat 10-5, Sun 10-2;
Oct-Apr, Mon-Fri 9-5, Sat 1-2. Guided tours.

Toppesfield Hall
Hadleigh
Tel: 0473 822922
May-Sept, Mon-Fri 9-5.15; May 27-Sept 2,
Sat 10-4.

Hotels

Maison Talbooth
Stratford Road
Dedham
Colchester
Tel: 0206 322367
Owned by the Milsom family with a long reputation for first class cuisine and luxurious accommodation. The Maison is a Victorian country house with views over the river.
Rooms: 10
Credit cards: Access, Visa, Diners, Amex
Rating ★★★★★

Dedham Vale Hotel
Stratford Road
Dedham
Colchester
Tel: 0206 322752
Small hotel in three acres of gardens, also owned by the Milsom family. The Terrace Restaurant serves smorgasbord and rotisserie meals.
Rooms: 6

Credit cards: Access, Visa, Diners, Amex
Rating ★★★★★

Hintlesham Hall
Hintlesham
nr Ipswich
Tel: 0473 87334
Made internationally famous by Robert Carrier, Hintlesham, now under different ownership, remains a much-loved retreat for London's monied classes. The house, in 18 acres of grounds, dates from the 16th century but has an added Georgian façade. It is the food – classic English and French – which attracts return visitors year after year. Clay pigeon shooting, riding and tennis are available, and the hall organises a regular round of weekend activities throughout the year, including trips to the races and cookery classes.
Rooms: 17
Credit cards: Access, Visa, Diners, Amex
Rating ★★★★★

Marlborough Hotel
Henley Road
Ipswich
Tel: 0473 57677
Rooms: 22
Credit cards: Access, Visa, Diners, Amex
Rating ★★★★

Belstead Brook
Belstead Road
Ipswich
Tel: 0473 684241
Rooms: 33
Credit cards: Access, Visa, Diners, Amex
Rating ★★★★

Private Accommodation

The Old Vicarage
Higham
nr Colchester
Tel: 020 637 248
Tudor country house with tennis court and swimming pool, close to Le Talbooth and

The Old Vicarage contd
Hintlesham Hall. No dinner facilities.
Rooms: 4
Credit cards: none
Rating ★★★

Elm House
14 Upper Holt Street
Earls Colne
Tel: 078 75 2197
Queen Anne house ten miles from
Colchester and 30 minutes drive from the
coast.
Rooms: 3
Credit cards: none
Rating ★★

Restaurants

Le Talbooth
Gun Hill
Dedham
Colchester
Tel: 0206 323150
Famous haute cuisine restaurant housed in
a picturesque building seen in Constable's
famous painting, *Dedham Vale*, now in the
National Gallery of Scotland.
Credit cards: Access, Visa, Diners, Amex
Rating ★★★★★

Historic Houses

Christchurch Mansion
Ipswich
Tudor mansion in central park with
paintings by Gainsborough, Constable and
other local artists. Mon-Sat 10-5, Sun 2.30-
4.30.

Gardens

Thompson & Morgan Seed Trials
Poplar Lane
London Road
Ipswich
One of East Anglia's leading seed
merchants shows off its exotic plant
collections. Mid Jul-end Sept, daily 9-4.

The Rosarium
Lime Kiln
Claydon
3m NW Ipswich
More than 400 varieties of rose, many of
them rare, and old. Garden at its best in the
first two weeks of June. May-Jul, daily 2-7.

East Bergholt Lodge
East Bergholt
9m NE Colchester
Tel: 0206 298278.
Richly stocked woodland garden, plants for
sale. May-Jun, some Suns, otherwise by
appointment.

Blakenham Woodland Garden
Little Blakenham
4m NW Ipswich
Lovely walks on five acre woodland garden
with rare trees. Apr-Sept, Wed, Thur, Sun
and Bank Hols, 1-5.

Museums

Ipswich Museum
Ipswich
Local history, bird life and 'mankind
galleries' from around the world. Mon-Sat
10-5.

Colchester and Essex Museum
Colchester Castle
Colchester
The city's claim to be Britain's first Roman
capital is substantiated in the collections
inside the museum, housed in the castle's
Norman keep. Apr-Sept, Mon-Sat 10-5, Sun
2.30-5; winter, Mon-Fri 10-5, Sat 10-4.

Tymperley Clock Museum
Tymperleys
Trinity Street
Colchester
Examples of some of the fine clock making
skills of past Colchester craftsmen. Apr-Oct,
Tues-Sat 10-1, 2-5.

Hollytrees
High St
Colchester
Historic costumes and social displays in
18th-century house. Mon-Sat 10-1, 2-5.

Museum of Natural History
All Saints Church
Colchester
Local natural history. Mon-Sat 10-1, 2-5.

Social History Museum
Holy Trinity Church
Colchester
Rural life and crafts. Mon-Sat, 10-1, 2-5.

Wildlife Parks and Reserves

Colchester Zoo
Colchester
Family zoo with animals, birds, reptiles and
aquaria, miniature railway, gardens and
amusements. All year, daily 9.30-5 or dusk.

Index

EAST ANGLIA